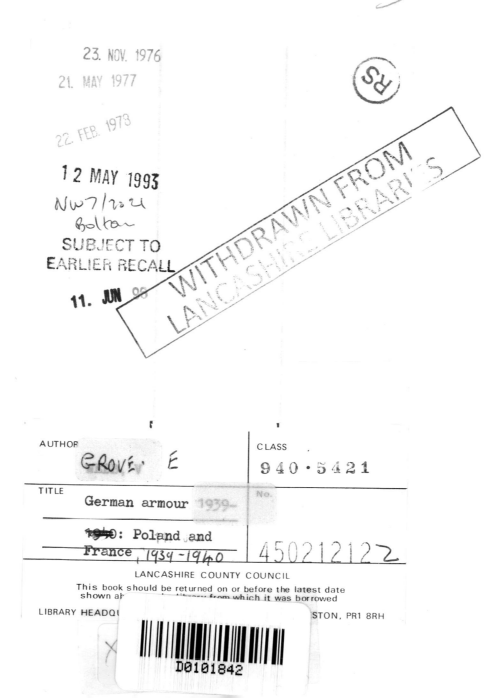

German Armour
Poland and France
1939-1940

by
Eric Grove

colour illustrations by
The Allard Design Group

Almark Publishing Co Ltd London

First Published 1976.

ISBN 0 85524 260 4

Distributed in the U. S. A. by
Squadron/Signal Publications Inc.,
3515, East Ten Mile Road,
Warren, Michigan 48091.

Printed in Great Britain by
Edwin Snell Printers,
Park Road, Yeovil,
Somerset,
for the publishers, Almark Publishing Co. Ltd.
49 Malden Way, New Malden,
Surrey KT3 6EA, England.

Contents

Acknowledgements

All pictures with the exception of those listed below are from the Imperial War Museum collection. Pages 20, 22, 23, 33, 41, 44, 45, 50, 52, 59, 62, 63, 64, 65, 67, 68 Almark.

Introduction

German Armour Poland and France by Eric Grove takes the reader from the origins of Germany's tank arm to its triumph over the Allies in 1940. The book covers the types available to the Wehrmacht in 1939 and shows how they were used in novel tactics to break through the static defences of the Polish and French armies.

A comprehensive postscript lists the tanks and their development history and shows that some of the types available were under-gunned and under-armoured by the standards of 1940.

PzKpfw 38(t) tanks of
Rommel's 7th Panzer
Division on the move
in France in 1940. In
the top and left of the
picture are the frame
antenna and MG34 of
Rommel's half-track.

The Eve of War

The German invasion of Poland on 1 September 1939 found the *Panzerwaffe* (Armoured Force) still in process of evolution and unprepared for war. In late 1938, Guderian was appointed Chief of Mobile Troops, with Hitler's personal backing, and given wide, if ill defined, powers over tanks, cavalry and motorised infantry. Guderian's appointment tilted the balance of influence in the Army High Command in favour of progressive armoured doctrine. This was the employment of full scale Panzer (armoured) Divisions with a balanced proportion of all arms but based around tanks and moving at their speed. Hitler had long seen these units as a vital component of the *Blitzkrieg* (lightning war) strategy that would gain him the domination of Europe without the casualties of 1914-18. Nevertheless as the German Army grew with rearmament, the strength of the traditional infantry and cavalry arms had been able to secure considerable dispersion of armoured strength. Two Panzer Brigades and a Panzer Regiment were formed as independent infantry support units, and four Light Divisions were assembled for cavalry duties, each with a battalion of light tanks submerged under four battalions of *Kavallerie Schützen* (cavalry riflemen) and a reconnaissance regiment. Guderian's immediate priority was to get these units reorganised but the process was incomplete when mobilisation orders came for the attack in the East. Plans were laid in early 1939 for the upgrading of the Light Divisions to full Panzer status; new 10th Panzer Division began to be formed in April around Panzer Regiment 8, one of the two regiments of the independent 4th Panzer Brigade. By September it was still not up to full strength, particularly in tanks. Upgrading the Light Divisions had not officially taken place but 1st and 3rd were mobilised with extra armour in the shape of Panzer Regiments 11 and 25 respectively – the two halves of the erstwhile 6th independent Panzer Brigade. This converted the two Light Divisions into Panzer Divisions in all but name. An even more ad hoc armoured division was formed by mobilising 4th Panzer Brigade H.Q. with Panzer Regiment 7 together with the S.S. *Standarte Deutschland* (motorised infantry regiment), the S.S. Artillery Regiment and Reconnaissance Battalion and some Army anti-tank and engineer troops. These were deployed in East Prussia, joining the local independent tank unit, 1st Battalion, Panzer Regiment 10, as *Panzerverband Ostpreussen*, sometimes known as *Panzerverband* Kempf after its commander.

The standard Panzer Division of late 1939 was a powerful, mobile force well trained by many exercises. The first three divisions had been in existence since 1935 and the other two had been formed in 1938. Each division had a brigade of two tank regiments and complementary motorised units of infantry and artillery. Except for a few half-track armoured

In a pre-war exercise a Panzerbefehlswagen I drives down a country road. The commander is wearing the early Panzer beret to which is attached a coloured band to indicate which side he is on in the exercise.

personnel carriers in 1st and 2nd Panzer Divisions all support vehicles were wheeled, although there were a few tracked ammunition carriers based on the PzKpfw I Ausf A. Each tank regiment was divided into two battalions, each of which in turn was composed of three companies of about 24 tanks each. Originally these companies had all been 'light' but in 1939 the increasing availability of the PzKpfw IV allowed one company in each battalion to be designated first 'mixed' and then 'medium'. The 1st Panzer Division, as the senior armoured unit, had the most impressive battalion tank establishment with 14 PzKpfw IVs (see appendix for details), 28 PzKpfw IIIs, 18 PzKpfw IIs and 17 PzKpfw Is and *Panzerbefehlswagen* (command vehicles). Including regimental H.Q. vehicles this amounted to 162 tanks per regiment, 324 for the division as a whole. The other four divisions had to make do with only six PzKpfw IVs and five PzKpfw IIIs per battalion to balance 33 PzKpfw IIs and 34 PzKpfw Is and *Panzerbefehlswagen* making a total of 164 tanks per regiment, 328 per division.

These figures, however, seem to have been notional rather than real due to the parlous state of German tank development and production. Neither the 37mm armed PzKpfw III, the projected backbone of the light companies nor the heavy fire support 75mm PzKpfw IV medium had been officially adopted for service. The design of the latter tank had been more or less finalised but enormous difficulties had been encountered in developing the suspension for the PzKpfw III. A definitive unit had only just been adopted after four years' work. A few IIIs had been completed as unarmed command tanks and there were only 98 pre-production PzKpfw III battle tanks available for action on 1 September. Some of these were with the *Panzer Lehr* Battalion, the special demonstration and training unit attached to Guderian's XIX Corps. Ninety-eight tanks were insufficient even to equip 1st Panzer Division up to its establishment of PzKpfw IIIs, and all units were very short supplied. There were 211 PzKpfw IVs which was just sufficient for medium tank requirements although the distribution of these even more valuable vehicles was hardly lavish.

This tardy rearmament reflected the German failure, repeated throughout the war, to recognise that 'the best is the enemy of the good'. The highly bureaucratic system of weapons procurement limited tank construction to a few established firms, such as Krupp, with limited expertise in the mass production of motor vehicles. Most important of all, the failure fully to mobilise the economy greatly hindered the war effort. Whatever the reasons, the *Panzerwaffe* were forced to rely on the light PzKpfw I and II for the major part of their strength. Designed for training, the military capabilities of these tanks were limited. The PzKpfw I was only armed with machine-guns, its 13mm armour was only sufficient protection against small arms and its cross country mobility was limited. The PzKpfw II was rather better with its armour piercing 20mm gun, frontal protection up to the 30mm standards of the PzKpfw III and IV and adequate mobility. However it

was hardly a powerful tank even by contemporary standards and was only intended as a stop gap until the PzKpfw III arrived. Production of the PzKpfw I and II had been quite high, and there were 1,445 and 1,223 of each respective type available for service, enough to fill out the strength of the variously deployed tank battalions.

Given these shortages of quality armour, the Germans had received a very useful windfall when they occupied Czecho-Slovakia in March. The Czech Army had been building up its tank strength with some remarkably effective vehicles, the Skoda LT-35 and the CKD/Praga LT-38. Although officially 'light' both these 37.2mm armed tanks were much more capable than the native German PzKpfw II and were directly comparable with the PzKpfw III. There were 298 LT-35s and 80 LT-38s available when the Germans invaded. Most were passed to the satellite Slovak Army, but there were enough LT-35s immediately to re-equip Panzer Regiment 11 and 1st Light Division's *Panzer Abteilung* 65 on an establishment of 17 per light company. The reinforced 1st Light Division, therefore, entered the

During the same exercise an SdKfz 231 and an SdKfz 232 armoured car drive past a horse-drawn field kitchen. The SdKfz 231 was armed with a 2cm KwK gun similar to the PzKpfw II.

A PzKpfw I Ausf A SdKfz 101 on a pre-war parade. The PzKpfw I was armed with two machine guns and had a crew of two.

Polish campaign as one of the Wehrmacht's most powerful armoured units.

Such then was the state of the *Panzerwaffe* when directed to its mobilisation stations along the Polish border. Despite its lack of proper equipment and the scratch nature of some of its units, the troops were better trained in the techniques of massed employment of armour and mobile all arms co-operation than any other in the world. Morale was high even though they were about to face a large army of 30 infantry divisions and 11 cavalry brigades. By the standards of World War I these should have been enough to stand a good chance of holding Germany's 41 available divisions. But this was not 1914. Ten of the Wehrmacht's divisions were armoured in one way or another and the ability of such units to change both the pace and face of war was about to have a spectacular demonstration.

The First Blitzkrieg

The German High Command gave its armoured forces the task of spearheading the double envelopment from north and south that was to trap and destroy the Polish forces in front of the Narev and Vistula rivers. Most of the armour was concentrated in the south with von Rundstedt's Army Group A, whose 10th Army was given the central role of driving on Warsaw. This included XV Motorised Corps with 2nd and 3rd Light Divisions (the former reinforced) and XVI Panzer Corps – still officially known as Army Corps (motorised) – with 1st and 4th Panzer Divisions. The reinforced 1st Light Division with its Czech tanks was allocated from Army Reserve to provide the cutting edge of the XIV Motorised Corps. To the right of 10th Army was 14th with the vital role of taking Cracow and advancing through Galicia to the San as quickly as possible, so turning the left flank of any attempted Polish defence. The 14th Army included the VIII Corps with 5th Panzer Division, and the XXII Panzer Corps with 2nd Panzer and 4th Light Divisions.

The other arm of the strategic pincers designed to outflank and destroy the Polish Army was von Bock's Army Group B. In East Prussia the weak 3rd Army had only Kempf's *Panzerverband* to reinforce its infantry and cavalry striking south to the Vistula and the Bug. Kluge's stronger 4th Army, which included Guderian's Panzer Corps with 3rd Panzer Division (reinforced at Guderian's request by the *Panzer Lehr* Battalion), had the task of cutting the Polish Corridor from west to east. The 10th Panzer Division was allocated as Army Reserve and deployed with a second line infantry division on Guderian's left. After cutting the Corridor these forces were to join with 3rd Army in its advance.

The attack got under way in the early hours of 1 September. Initially there was little opposition and the major problems were created by bogged down PzKpfw Is having to be recovered by other tanks. The southern offensive, however, soon ran into difficulties against the Polish defences. The Wolynska Cavalry Brigade, fighting skilfully, used their 37mm anti-tank guns and anti-tank rifles to good effect and held 4th Panzer Division for two days. All the German tanks were, to some extent, vulnerable to Polish anti-tank weapons and in these initial combats against prepared positions, tanks and infantry fought on almost equal terms. Armour sometimes had a limited role to play, as when the 3rd *Kavallerie Schützen* Battalion of 1st Light Division was stalled on the marshy approaches to the River Warta on 3 September. The infantry commander was beginning to lose heart but his resolution was stiffened by Colonel Koll, the commander of the nearest Panzer Battalion. He offered a company of PzKpfw 35(t)s to assist the assault by leading the infantry through the navigable paths in front of the river. The tanks covered the assault with their 37.2mm guns and drew

PzKpfw Is ford a stream. The crew are wearing the characteristic black uniforms of Panzer troops and the black beret which was discontinued after the 1939 campaign.

the Polish machine-gun fire away from the infantry advancing behind them. Unfortunately for the Germans the river was too deep to ford and, while the infantry secured the crossing, the tanks had to be used to drag bogged down vehicles out of the marsh.

In fact it was only the advance of the unarmoured 8th Army which unhinged the Polish defences and forced their High Command to order a general withdrawal to the Vistula on the 5th. But once this began, the German armour came into its own as 10th Army's two

Panzer and three Light Divisions raced forward to the Vistula cutting off the less mobile Poles. The tanks moved quickly forward through sporadic Polish resistance. Little mercy was shown to the Poles who fought back, so building up an aura of powerful invincibility around the tanks that had a considerable morale effect. Against unprotected infantry all types of tanks could use their weapons to formidable effect. Enemy positions in trenches could be physically crushed and when even fortified machine-gun nests were encountered it usually fell to the medium companies' PzKpfw IVs to destroy them with high explosive fire. The support provided by these tanks was even more important against anti-tank guns and enemy artillery. The well trained tank crews were able to switch targets flexibly as they variously presented themselves. Radio communication allowed co-ordinated attacks. Light running repairs, such as changing damaged track shoes, were carried out on the march, while supplies were given top priority to keep the tanks on the move.

The reliance on the more heavily gunned tanks to provide fire support showed that the tank brigades were now outrunning their infantry and other support units. The tanks indeed were sometimes forced to halt to allow their infantry to catch up to assist in the assault of particularly well defended positions. This made the tanks particularly vulnerable to artillery and anti-tank guns, directed by observers left behind among the advancing German tanks. The German Panzer crews quickly learnt that movement was their greatest defence, although some tanks proved surprisingly tough, one PzKpfw IV taking three 37mm gun and several anti-tank rifle hits without being knocked out.

The Poles lacked a mobile counter to the German armour. Their small, machine-gun armed TK and TKS tankettes, widely distributed among the infantry divisions and cavalry brigades, proved vulnerable even to the PzKpfw II's 20mm fire. In one recorded tank versus tank combat, a small tankette was riddled with five out of six of the shells from the PzKpfw II's second burst of fire. Only the few tankettes with 20mm guns could, and did, strike back in kind. Heavier Polish armour existed in only small quantities, and its limited counter-attacks could be held by German anti-tank defences, as when 12 37mm armed 7TPs were knocked out on 9 September near Warsaw by 37mm anti-tank guns of 4th Panzer Division. These modern Polish tanks were good machines by contemporary German standards, if a little lightly armoured (only

Above: A PzKpfw pulls off a country track into a field. The tank has a spare road wheel stowed behind the turret.
Left: A PzKpfw II. With better sloped armour and a heavier gun the II was an improvement on the PzKpfw I, but it was still under armed compared to the tanks it would meet in the West.

A PzKpfw IV Ausf D is ferried across a river on a pontoon raft. The tank has a stack of logs attached to the turret for use in unditching from soft ground.

17mm) and captured examples were pressed into service by German formations, eg 1st Light Division.

Despite such successes, resistance became more severe as the Panzers approached Warsaw. On 8 September a small dug-in Polish force of 37mm anti-tank guns, 75 mm field artillery and 7TP tanks inflicted heavy casualties on one group of advancing Panzers destroying up to 40 of them. The next day 4th Panzer Division reached the southern streets of Warsaw and quickly found again that armour was not the answer to all tactical situations. Although they could drive through fences and wooden sheds, the more substantial buildings soon channelled the tanks into predictable lanes covered by anti-tank weapons and field artillery or protected by minefields. The aura of invincibility that the Panzers had built up caused the Poles to abandon their extended positions but, as the German tanks moved towards the city centre, they became split up and vulnerable even to grenade attacks. The few available PzKpfw IVs could reply to direct fire artillery on equal terms, but these tanks were still vulnerable to concentrated anti-tank fire. The 20mm guns and machine-guns of the PzKpfw I and II could explode enemy gun's ammunition supplies or shoot exposed defenders, but they could not physically destroy from a distance the heavier enemy weapons. Eventually after five hours, the damaged survivors had to call a halt and withdraw, picking up those crewmen of the knocked out tanks who remained alive. The regiment which mounted the assault lost about half of the 120 tanks with which it started the day.

To the south Germans were having a more successful time as the Light Divisions and motorised infantry of XIV and XV Motorised

Corps closed around Radom trapping three Polish infantry divisions. The Light Division had advanced 800 kilometres (497 miles) in eight days cutting off Radom from the south. On 9 September the Division mounted an assault on Ilza to complete the encirclement. Laying down a heavy fire from their 37.2mm guns and machine-guns, the leading companies of PzKpfw 35(t)s attacked through the fire of Polish anti-aircraft guns and anti-tank rifles. The latter proved rather ineffective against the Skodas' 28-35 armour, and even flame-throwers were used by the Poles in defence. Some German tanks were knocked out, but the remainder reached their objective, the vital crossroads on the road east to the River Bug at Pulway. Some surrounded Polish troops broke out but 60,000 were taken prisoner.

However, a crisis was then developing to the north. The Polish Pomorze and Poznan Armies, trapped by the German strategic thrusts from the north and south, were trying to break out of their trap. They mounted strong attacks along the Bzura on 9 September against the exposed flanks of the German infantry of 8th Army. As pressure grew, the Germans swung XIV Panzer Corps from Warsaw and ordered 1st Light Division up from Radom. Despite 4th Panzer Division's losses, the other two armoured units were the two most powerful in the German Army and their mobility allowed their quick deployment to the critical area. They presented a powerful obstacle to the south and west of the cut-off Poles whose armour had been abandoned for lack of fuel further north. Counter-attacks were mounted to thrust the Poles back north of the Bzura in which the weakness of the lighter German tanks, particularly those of the PzKpfw I, was again shown. One company had great problems with its vehicles bogging down.

A Czech (Skoda) LT-35 S2A. Taken over by the Germans these tanks were known as PzKpfw 35(t). The (t) stood for *tsceche*, the German for Czech.

A PzKpfw IV Ausf C. The B and C were very similar, both had a straight frontal plate with double driver's visor and pistol port and peep slot instead of a bow machine gun.

Despite such setbacks, pressure began to tell on the encircled Poles as infantry of the German 4th Army pushed southwards. A final break-out was attempted to the east but the Light Divisions of XV Motorised Corps were rushed in from Radom to close the gap. Resistance ceased on the 18th and, although some Poles managed to escape, 170,000 were taken prisoner. However without the German ability quickly to redeploy mobile armoured units, the story might well have been different.

By that time the two furthest German armoured pincers were beginning to close behind the Vistula and San. As with 10th Army both the tank equipped Corps of 14th Army faced problems in the initial phase. The VIII Corps, in taking the northern route to Cracow, was given considerable trouble by the frontier defences. PzKpfw I and II were hardly assault tanks. Despite some imaginative overnight manoeuvring through difficult country by von Thoma's 2nd Panzer Brigade

of 2nd Panzer Division, XXII Panzer Corps ran into difficulties with Poland's only fully operational mechanised unit. This was the 10th Cavalry Brigade, which deployed 47mm armed VAU33 tanks, 37mm anti-tank guns, 75mm field guns and 100mm medium artillery and had been specially intended as an anti-tank unit. Only force of numbers prevailed, but this opened the way for another Panzer thrust. The 10th Cavalry's mobile actions helped prevent a disastrous encirclement at Cracow. However, 14th Army's two Panzer Divisions and one Light Division crossed the San and by the time the Bzura battle was ending the Poles were throwing their last armoured units against XXII Panzer Corps at Tomaszow Lubelski to try to keep open the Polish escape route from Warsaw to the north. Despite some limited Polish gains these attempts were abandoned by 20 September.

Coming down from the north on the other side of the Polish escape route were the tanks of XIX Panzer Corps under Guderian. His Corps had crossed into the Polish Corridor from the west on the opening day of the offensive. The Polish defences near the border did not prove very strong and most of Guderian's immediate difficulties were caused by his own troops. Leading from the front in his command half-track he was almost killed by his own artillery on the misty morning of the first day. His forces also proved a little battle shy and had to be urged on personally by their aggressive commander. Due to this prodding, momentum was built up which proved decisive. The Pomorska Cavalry Brigade showed more courage than common sense in attacking 3rd Panzer Division's tanks with sabres and lances, only to be mown down. Polish anti-tank guns proved more troublesome and PzKpfw IVs had to be used against them, one tank under cover of a smoke screen destroying three badly disposed weapons with a single 75mm shell. The tanks drove through the Corridor's forest paths, scattering fire in all directions. This, plus the failure of their cavalry, caused general Polish demoralisation and the disintegration of their forces. The Poles were not given any chance to stabilise a new line. Defences were over-run even as they were built, destroyed by gunfire or crushed under the tanks' tracks. Bridges were captured before they were blown. A train of Polish reserves on its way to the front line was even 'held up' by a PzKpfw IV whose commander, Lieutenant von Krause, was thus presented with 400 surprised prisoners. By the 4th, XIX Panzer Corps, with 3rd Panzer Division in the lead, had cut the Corridor and was mopping up the remains of the Polish defenders.

The plan was then to join 3rd Army's advance towards the Narew and Vistula which had already begun successfully. Guderian's tanks were seen as useful support for this offensive towards Warsaw. However, the ar-

chitect of Germany's armoured forces saw richer pickings further east in the direction of Brest Litovsk, out-flanking any Polish defence behind Warsaw. Authorisation to carry out this drive was given by Army Group South on 8 September and XIX Corps was reinforced with 10th Panzer Division. The latter's raw units needed prompting from Guderian during the crossing of the Narew. Great confusion was caused when 20th Motorised Division commandeered the bridges set up to carry the tanks of the two Panzer Divisions across the river. The 10th and 3rd Panzer Divisions were forced to use ferries to get their ranks across. Despite these setbacks and some stiff Polish resistance, Guderian's forces pressed southwards with 3rd Panzer Division on the left, 10th Panzer in the centre and 20th Motorised Division reinforced with parts of 10th Panzer Division on the right. By the 15th Brest Litovsk was surrounded to the east. A single Polish World War I vintage Renault FT17 tank blocking the gate of the old citadel foiled 10th Panzer Division's tanks attempting

A PzKpfw II on the Aisne in 1940. The chassis of the PzKpfw II was used for a variety of self-propelled guns and tank destroyers, and there were even experiments with an amphibious version for the proposed invasion of Britain.

An unusual view of a PzKpfw IV Ausf C. The crew are wearing the black side cap, but the driver has retained the panzer berret. To the left of the gun is the machine gun in its armoured jacket.

a surprise attack. Brest finally fell to XIX Panzer Corps infantry on 17 September.

By then 3rd Panzer had advanced further to the south to cut off any Poles retreating to the east. On the 16th the Division formed a *Gruppe Wandenburg* from a combination of 1st Battalion, 5th Panzer Regiment with a motor-cycle company, a battery of artillery and half a platoon of engineers. It was to press on ahead to cut the main Polish line of retreat from Lublin to Kovel at Przewo, where road and railway bridges crossed the River Bug. Picking up the motor-cyclists on the way, but not waiting for the artillery, the tanks set out in the evening. The motor-cyclists soon bogged down on the sandy roads but the tanks kept on into the night and moved through the densely forested territory with men on the outside, assisted by 'drafted' locals, using headlights to pick out navigable paths. Such a nocturnal advance through difficult country

was typical of the 'press on' spirit which had stood the Panzers in good stead throughout the campaign.

Opposition was not severe as the Poles were by then in great confusion, but fuel was becoming a problem in such an advanced position. It was decided, therefore, to push ahead two scouting troops each of one or two PzKpfw IVs and two or three PzKpfw IIIs to carry out the mission. (This division seems to have secured more than its fair share of PzKpfw IIIs.) One group drove to Przewo shooting up retreating Polish columns met on the way. So many prisoners were taken that two PzKpfw IIIs had to be left to guard them. Arriving in Przewo the engineers riding in the three remaining tanks dismounted to set fire to the wooden road bridge. Abandoning the idea of taking more prisoners, the tanks pressed on to the railway. The strain of many miles was beginning to tell and one PzKpfw IV now broke down with suspension problems. With the help of some captured men and vehicles this tank eventually made it back to the battalion. Nothing daunted, the surviving vehicles, guided by a local, pushed on to the railway line which was blown up. A double-headed train coming west was also stopped by 75mm and 37mm shells. The tanks then decided to return since the remaining PzKpfw IV's Maybach engine was also beginning to show the strain. They fought off an artillery attack using their own gunfire and a smoke screen. The tanks then came under heavy machine-gun and rifle fire which did not penetrate but killed, or severely wounded, all the Polish prisoners clinging to the commander's PzKpfw IV. The only exterior survivor was the German radio operator who had given up his place to a wounded engineer. The inside of this tank was so crowded with the extra engineers that the loader had his arm broken by the recoil of the gun but he continued to load with his left hand. As the tank

A PzBefWg III slides into the crater formed by demolitions during fighting in France. The tank however still has the white cross which was the insignia worn in the Polish campaign. Visible behind the turret is the frame antenna for the extra radio carried in this command vehicle.

battalion had moved some distance south to keep in contact, the two tanks had just enough fuel to reach safety. The other scouting group had similar success blowing up the line and stopping another train with gunfire.

At 16.00 on 17 September a full attack was ordered, air reconnaissance having reported traffic still moving east through Przewo. Refuelling was completed within the hour and, again not waiting for support, the battalion advanced, one PzKpfw IV being deployed with the light 2nd Company on the left to strengthen it. This tank was able to push through to the railway on its own where it found one of the trains still stopped, although attempts had been made to re-open the line. The battalion commander was beginning to feel a little exposed as night came on, his tanks standing out in sharp relief in the light of the burning village and forest. A retreat was ordered to the original jumping off point while the 8th battalion, 3rd Motorised Rifle Regiment, came up to guard the tanks and deploy forward to consolidate the ground won.

On the 18th the tanks advanced once more to find that most of the Poles had crossed the Bug. The railway bridge, damaged by the Luftwaffe but patched up by the Poles, was finally blown. The Panzers, together with the infantry and artillery, held the position under artillery fire, expecting a battle with retreating Poles, but the Germans were eventually withdrawn to the east on the 19th. The hoped-for link up with 14th Army never came, because Russian forces moved in claiming their portion of Poland under the terms of the previous month's Soviet-German pact. Guderian's Corps was to withdraw from the area by 22 September.

With the Polish Government interned in Romania it only remained to bombard

19

German infantry slump beside the road after days of marching. The infantry were vital in Blitzkrieg operations since they reduced strong points which had been bypassed by the tanks and also secured the ground behind the tanks.

Warsaw into surrender on the 28th. The lesson of 4th Panzer Division's 'bloody nose' three weeks before had been learned and the task of closely investing the city was given to the infantry of 8th Army. On 6 October the last significant Polish forces surrendered. A country had been conquered for the cost of only 217 tanks irreparably destroyed – although considerably more were knocked out and later repaired. Poland with a potential army of 2.5 million had been totally defeated for the loss of 8,000 German lives, an almost trivial number by World War I standards. Tanks were not the only factor in victory. Air power had played a decisive part, but in the final analysis it was the tanks of the Panzer and Light Divisions which actually out-manoeuvred the Poles. This had prevented a trench-war developing which would have given time for the Poles to shake themselves out of their confusion and fully mobilise their forces. Guderian's ideas had been fully vindicated.

Reorganisation and Re-equipment

Hitler's invasion of Poland had landed him, perhaps rather earlier than he would have liked, with the war with Britain and France that he had long expected. He then wished to go ahead as quickly as possible in October with the assault in the west. This would have meant that the *Panzerwaffe* would have had no time to get over the strains of its first combats or fully absorb the Polish campaign's many useful lessons. Luckily for them the date was soon put back to November and then the weather led to a series of further delays until January when the plans for the offensive fell into Allied hands causing a final postponement until spring.

So the opportunity was obtained to complete the reorganisation of the Light Divisions on the basis planned before Poland and vindicated under combat conditions. In October 1st and 2nd Light Divisions, which had fought in Poland as Panzer divisions in all but name, were redesignated 6th and 7th Panzer Divisions. The Light Divisions' tank battalions were incorporated in the 11th and 25th Panzer Regiments respectively, now organic parts of their respective divisions. At the same time the East Prussian 10th Panzer Regiment, now two full battalions, absorbed the 3rd Light Division's 67th Tank Battalion to create the tank component of 7th Panzer Division. The 4th Light continued until January 1940 when Germany's last available free tank unit, the *Panzer Lehr* Battalion joined the division to create the small 33rd Panzer Regiment of 9th Panzer Division. The 10th Panzer Division also completed its assembly, reuniting under 4th Panzer Brigade H.Q. the 7th and 8th Panzer Regiments after the former's sojourn with the S.S. The Division also got its full complement of infantry and Panzer Divisions 1 to 4 also had this component increased. Poland had shown that tanks and infantry were mutually dependent, although the construction of proper armoured personnel carriers remained as slow as ever.

It was the same for other tracked support vehicles. One or two self-propelled 150mm infantry guns mounted on the PzKpfw I Ausf B chassis were available for use in Poland. Although useful as heavy fire support for advanced mobile units, their construction stopped after only 38 vehicles, enough for only six Panzer Divisions to be equipped with a company of six guns each. A new self-propelled vehicle based on the same chassis, a tank destroyer mounting the Czech 47mm gun, only entered production in March 1940. This gave a little extra power and significantly greater mobility to motorised anti-tank battalions but only 92 were completed in the next two months and the type was only just coming into service when the Western campaign began. PzKpfw I Ausf A and B chassis were also being used as armoured engineer vehicles and mobile transport for Panzer repair units but, given the numbers available of this

A PzKpfw III Ausf D on a road in France. Visible to the right of the driver's slit is the divisional insignia of the 5th Panzer.

the infantry would be without armoured support. Based on World War I experience of direct fire artillery (*Sturmgeschütze* – assault guns) for close support for the infantry, the artillery arm had begun development in 1936 of an armoured 75mm self-propelled *Sturmgeschütz* on the PzKpfw III Ausf B chassis. Five prototypes of these turretless tanks had been built but in 1938 development stopped, perhaps because the always rather conservative artillerymen considered that these vehicles were 'tanks' rather than guns. Poland, however, re-affirmed the need for such a vehicle and in February 1940 30 pre-production *Sturmgeschütze* were ordered, enough for five batteries. The first gun, based on the latest PzKpfw III chassis, was delivered in April and only one battery was ready for action in May. The infantry would have to do without armoured support.

Most crucial of all, however, tank production still lagged. Of the German tanks lost in Poland 150 had been PzKpfw Is and the Germans tried in vain to replace them with the much more powerful PzKpfw IIIs and IVs. At a meeting with Hitler on 5 September Guderian had asked for more of the two larger types, which were at long last officially accepted for service on the 27th of that month. Yet only 142 PzKpfw III tanks were completed between 1 September and the end of 1939, despite the virtual cessation of PzKpfw I and II production. Moreover the monthly rate of production did not increase as the attack in the west drew closer, although at least all the production Ausf F and G tanks were completed as combat rather than command vehicles. Both models were still equipped with the 37mm gun, although work was in progress to fit a more powerful 50mm weapon in a slightly modified turret. Given the shortage of PzKpfw IIIs it is surprising to find a reference to the production of 32 recovery vehicles on this chassis in 1939 and 34 the next

obsolete chassis, work along these lines was not carried out with much vigour.

Poland had shown that it was useless to group Panzer Divisions with conventional 'marching' infantry with their horse drawn support. But if all tanks were to be concentrated in Panzer Divisions this meant that

year. Although battlefield recovery and quick repair were crucial adjuncts to German tactical superiority it was perhaps rather self indulgent to convert or build new scarce tank chassis for this purpose when half-tracked heavy tractors were available.

Krupp continued to turn out PzKpfw IVs at a strangely lethargic pace: none in September, 20 in October, 11 in November, 14 in December. The story remained the same in 1940. Production was perhaps delayed then by the adoption of a new slightly improved model the Ausf D, proved necessary by the battles against Polish high velocity guns.

But such figures showed that German industry was still not exerting itself, despite the outbreak of general war. Germany had been in theory following a policy of 'guns before butter' since 1935. A production average of around 50 tanks per month makes an interesting comparison with the Allied monthly averages for 1943 of well over 1,000 for both the Sherman and T-34. The realities of a total war had yet to come to Germany. Hopefully *Blitzkrieg* would prevent them coming at all.

All this made Czech tank production even more vital. About 52 PzKpfw 35(t)s were built by the Germans between April 1939 and May 1940 and *circa* 218 of the simpler CKD/Praga

A PzKpfw 38(t). The 38(t) armed with two machine guns and a 3.7cm gun was a useful addition to the German armed forces and its chassis was the basis for a range of efficient tank destroyers in the latter part of the war.

A PzKpfw II leads a PzKpfw I during training in the severe winter of 1939-40. The tank is part of the 4th Panzer Division recognisable by the markings right of the driver's slit.

LT-38 tanks, designated PzKpfw 38(t). Some of these latter had been ordered from the Czechs by Sweden before the occupation but were seized for use by the Germans. The 6th Panzer Division had its light company tank establishment increased to 22 while the 38(t)s went to 7th- and 8th Panzer Divisions to provide a replacement for the PzKpfw IIIs. The Polish 7TP tanks remained in service for some months but were eventually withdrawn to Romania.

It was not to be through superiority in numbers or technology that victory would be gained in the west. Indeed, German A.F.V. production seems especially derisory when it is considered that she was planning an offensive against France, with her superiority in numbers of more heavily gunned and armoured tanks. Hitler, however, had gauged his opponent well. He saw that the internal weaknesses and irresolution of the French political and military leadership could be exploited by a new *Blitzkrieg*. Guderian would have liked more, and better, tanks but he too saw the fatal flaws of a military system based around the slow moving concepts of World War I. Hitler was gambling on Guderian's concepts working against numerical superiority, and the latter, given some Panzer units for training in the Eiffel mountains, set the pace, working the *Panzertruppen* hard to reach a new pitch of efficiency. But first, German attention moved to the north.

Scandinavian Diversion

In January 1940 planning began for the German invasion of Denmark and Norway. After some delay, the operation codenamed *Weserübung* (Weser Exercise) was set to begin on 9 April. Due to Norway's geographical position and terrain the armoured component of the *Blitzkrieg* would be less effective than in Poland but a special tank battalion, *Panzer Abteilung 40*, was formed to give a small armoured edge to the German attacks should there be serious opposition. This unit consisted of some 40 to 50 PzKpfw I Ausf A and B and PzKpfw II Ausf C tanks drawn from the 4th Panzer Division's 35th Panzer Regiment. Because no PzKpfw IVs could be spared, heavier weight was provided by three armoured *Neubaufahrzeug* (NbFz – New Construction Vehicle) prototypes. These were spectacular multi-turreted, but thinly protected, vehicles which had not been chosen for mass production. Despite their drawbacks they were armed with 75mm and 37mm guns and thus capable of providing some useful support for the lighter tanks. They also looked impressive in propaganda photographs which could reinforce the erroneous Allied belief in the qualitative superiority of the masses of modern tanks which had apparently crushed Poland.

The NbFz troop was sent to Oslo by sea, once the city had been secured, and pictures of this new 'PzKpfw V' in the streets caused a considerable stir in the British War Office. Contemporary Allied artists' impressions of

German tanks 'in action' usually showed quantities of these machines in the forefront. They did soon see some action, north of Oslo against Norwegian troops.

The rest of the battalion advanced through Denmark to Aalborg from whence it was shipped to Oslo on 17 April. By this time the first Allied forces were landing at Namsos and Aandalsnes to make a two pronged attack on Trondheim. The two battalions of the British 148th Infantry Brigade that landed at Aandalsnes were soon drawn south by the threat of stronger German forces. In order to back up the German *Gruppe* in this sector a small

A German infantry officer talks to the commander of a PzBefWg I during the invasion of Poland. This tank had no armament except for a machine gun, but it did have an extra 17mm of armour plate on the turret and 10mm on the nose.

A PzKpfw I Auf B SdKfz 101 1936 in Poland. The tank has the characteristic white crosses of that period and is finished in field grey. It had a Maybach NL 38 TR six cylinder water cooled engine, weighed 5.8 tons and. was armed with two machine-guns with a total of 3,125 rounds. Maximum armour was 13mm and minimum 7mm thick.

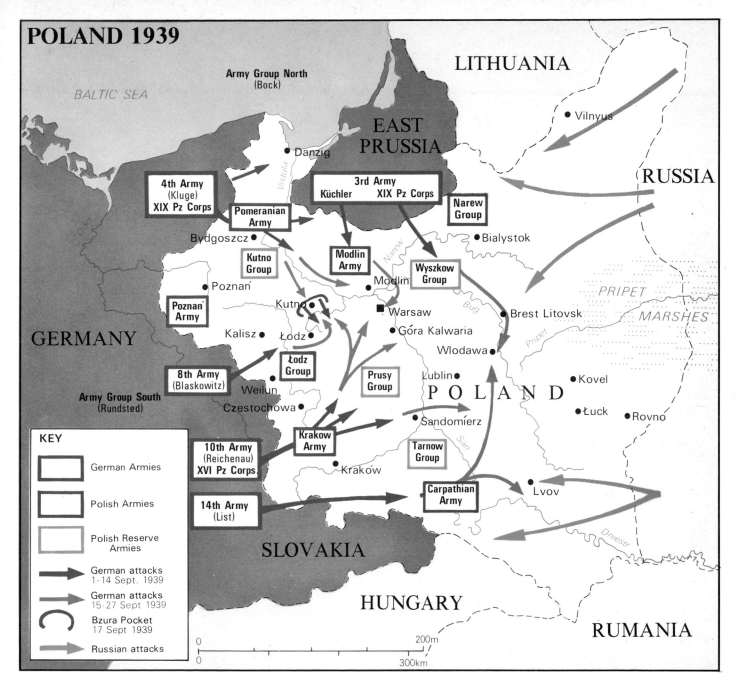

POLAND 1939

BALTIC SEA

LITHUANIA

RUSSIA

Army Group North
(Bock)

EAST PRUSSIA

Danzig

4th Army
(Kluge)
XIX Pz Corps

Pomeranian
Army

3rd Army
Küchler   XIX Pz Corps

Narew
Group

Vilnyus

Bydgoszcz

Kutno
Group

Modlin
Army

Bialystok

Wyszkow
Group

Narew

GERMANY

Poznań

Poznań
Army

Kutno

Modlin

Warsaw

Bug

Brest Litovsk

PRIPET
MARSHES

Pripet

Kalisz

Łódz

Łódz
Group

Prusy
Group

Góra Kalwaria

Wlodawa

Lublin

POLAND

Kovel

8th Army
(Blaskowitz)

Weilun

Czestochowa

Łuck

Rovno

Krakow
Army

Sandomierz

San

Tarnow
Group

Army Group South
(Rundsted)

KEY

German Armies

Polish Armies

Polish Reserve
Armies

German attacks
1-14 Sept. 1939

German attacks
15-27 Sept 1939

Bzura Pocket
17 Sept 1939

Russian attacks

10th Army
(Reichenau)
XVI Pz Corps

14th Army
(List)

Kraków

Carpathian
Army

Lvov

SLOVAKIA

Dniestr

HUNGARY

RUMANIA

0   200m

0   300km

27

Germany's propaganda bluff. The multi-turreted Neubaufahrzeuge (New Construction Vehicles) land at Oslo docks.

force of tanks, one NbFz, one PzKpfw II and four PzKpfw Is, was sent up to Lillehammer. There it went into action against the Anglo-Norwegian forces on the afternoon of 23 April. The British Boys anti-tank rifles, despite a theoretical penetration of 21mm of armour, proved ineffective against the German tanks. The first defensive position at Tretten, north of Lillehammer, was brushed aside, and the tanks crushed the log road block and

outflanked the infantry to the sides. The next day the process was repeated against the Norwegians to the north. In this difficult country a limited number of tanks could have a considerable effect as both battering rams and mobile cover. In the absence of effective Allied anti-tank weapons, the road north of Lillehammer could be used fully. Only the necessity to repair blown bridges limited the armoured advance.

The German *Gruppe*, now under General Pallengahr, moved on against stiffening resistance from the British 15th Infantry Brigade, which had been redeployed from France and was equipped with nine French 25mm anti-tank guns. Two German light tanks were destroyed trying to repeat the simple tactics of before, and it was the Group's artillery that now proved the decisive advantage. Two more tank troops had a rather easier time against the badly equipped Norwegians defending the more easterly route north from the German *Gruppe Fischer*. On 27 April the Allies decided to cut their losses in central Norway and by 3 May the evacuation was complete. The emphasis then shifted to the north where German armour was of little relevance.

It would be wrong to place too much stress on the activities of the small numbers of

Above: Captured French 25mm Hotchkiss anti-tank guns on display in 1940. This gun was small and light, and quite inadequate as an anti-tank weapon. *Left:* With two soldiers riding on the back a crew man of a PzKpfw II mounts his tank prior to driving down a railway track in Norway.

A PzKpfw 35(t) LTM-35 in Poland. The tank has a national flag draped over the rear deck for air identification. It was powered by a six cylinder water cooled in-line O.H.V. Skoda model T-11, 8.5L, developing 120 h.p. at 1,800 r.p.m. Armour thickness was between 35mm and 12mm and the tank was armed with one 37.2mm gun and two 7.92mm machine-guns.

A PzKpfw III Auf D SdKfz 141 in Poland. This tank was powered by a Maybach HL 108 TR V-12 engine, developing 320 h.p. at 3,000 r.p.m., and was armed with one 3.7cm gun and three 7.92mm machine-guns. It had a crew of five, a maximum speed of 40 k.p.h. and the addition of more armour put the weight up to 19.8 tons.

PzKpfw 38(t)s of
Rommel's 7th Panzer
Division on the move
in France. A platoon
of infantry can be
seen on the left
advancing in support
of the tanks.

German tanks in Norway. The German victory reflected a general superiority, not least in the air, which would anyway have proved decisive. Nevertheless the tanks added useful weight to the heterogeneous all arms groups which overcame the ill co-ordinated and badly led Allied resistance. As many problems were created by the terrain as by the enemy, one of the NbFz prototypes having to be blown up when it bogged down in the river bed it was trying to cross, so holding up troops to the rear.

Norway had seen German tanks used in a very traditional infantry support role. As the campaign drew to a close for the *Panzertruppen* in the north their comrades massing along Germany's western frontiers were about to demonstrate something more.

The Line Up for France

The original *Fall Gelb* (Case Yellow), drawn up by the German High Command for the campaign in the west, was unadventurous and conventional. Almost all the Panzer Divisions were to be used to lead a broad frontal attack by Army Group B through Holland and Belgium, the aim being to defeat 'the largest possible elements of the French and Allied armies and simultaneously gain as much territory as possible'. This unimaginative and unambitious strategy threw the strongest German forces against the strongest Allied and, even if successful, would have given only partial victory. It did not appeal to Hitler and was eventually replaced by Manstein's *Sichelschnitt* (Sickle Cut). This was a massive armoured *Schwerpunkt* (main thrust) through the Ardennes, where the French line least expected a major attack. Surprise and armoured mobility would cut off the most powerful Allied forces 'fixed' in the north by the diversionary attack of Army Group B. Once these forces had been cut off from their supply lines and destroyed, the Germans would be in a favourable position to deliver the coup de grâce.

So when the German forces moved up in May the centre of gravity had firmly shifted south. Guderian, a strong advocate of *Sichelschnitt*, had the central role with his XIX Panzer Corps. It was then composed of 1st, 2nd and 10th Panzer Divisions together with the crack Gross-Deutschland motorised infantry regiment which had the only available new

General von Manstein the man who planned the Sickle Cut phase of Case Yellow in the invasion of France.

Sturmgeschütz battery in support. This powerful Corps would strike at the junction of French 2nd and 9th Armies at Sedan and make the decisive breakthrough across the Meuse. To widen the gap Guderian's Corps was joined in *Panzergruppe* Kleist by Reinhardt's XLI Panzer Corps, composed of the Czech equipped 6th

A PzKpfw I Auf A SdKfz 101 in Norway. Armed with two machine-guns and with armour thickness between 13mm and 7mm the PzKpfw IAufA had a road speed of 37 k.p.h. The engine was a Krupp M 305 petrol engine rated at 57 h.p. at 2,500 r.p.m. It had a two man crew.

An NbFz A in action in Norway. This tank, one
of three prototypes, was armed with two
machine-guns in independent turrets and a third co-
axial with the main armament of a 75mm and a
37mm gun. It was powered by a Maybach HL 108
TR engine developing 280 h.p. It had a crew of six.

German paratroopers in action in Holland. Their attacks secured bridges and airfields and disrupted the Dutch defence.

Divisions. Höpner's XVI Panzer Corps with 3rd and 4th Panzer Divisions was to lead 6th Army's advance into central Belgium, while Schmidt's XXXIX Panzer Corps deployed 9th Panzer Division with other mobile units to spearhead 18th Army, and relieve the paratroops dropped on the Netherlands. Following the lessons of Poland when conventional 'marching' infantry with their horse-drawn supply wagons had failed to keep up with the tanks no such units were grouped with armour for the Western campaign.

As might be expected the positioning of these forces in the attack plan was reflected in their establishment composition. Guderian's 1st, 2nd and 10th Panzer Divisions were strongest in PzKpfw IIIs and IVs with 90 and 56 of each respectively; 100 PzKpfw II and 30 PzKpfw I light tanks filled out the theoretical strength of each division to 276 tanks. These formations were also equipped with armoured personnel half-tracks and self-propelled guns. Next, and arguably even stronger, came 6th, 7th and 8th Panzer Divisions with fewer tanks but a much larger proportion of 37mm armed vehicles: 132 PzKpfw 35(t)s or 38(t)s, 36 PzKpfw IVs, 40 PzKpfw IIs and 10 PzKpfw Is. Moving north 3rd, 4th and 5th Panzer Divisions had an establishment of 324 tanks, but these were mainly light: 140 PzKpfw Is and 110 PzKpfw IIs with 50 PzKpfw IIIs and 24 PzKpfw IVs. Finally 9th Panzer had only 18 PzKpfw IVs, 36 PzKpfw IIIs, 75 PzKpfw IIs and 100 PzKpfw Is, a total of 229.

These figures should only be used as a very general guide as tank establishments had been increased before the vehicles were available. There were only 381 PzKpfw IIIs and 290 PzKpfw IVs available for service at the beginning of May, 75 and 76 tanks below respective requirements. There were just enough PzKpfw 35(t)s with 143 on hand but there were only 238 PzKpfw 38(t)s against a requirement for

and 8th Panzer Divisions which would strike to the north around Monthermé. Although the two Corps were theoretically parts of the 16th and 12th Armies the *Panzergruppe* was meant to act as an autonomous unit under Army Group Control to score the decisive breakthrough. General Ewald von Kleist had commanded XXII Panzer Corps during the Polish campaign but as a rather conservative cavalryman he was no friend of Guderian's and had been appointed largely to keep the latter under control. Hoth's XV Panzer Corps with 7th and 5th Panzer Divisions was further north still with 4th Army completing the attack in the Ardennes and providing flank protection along the northern side of the projected 'Panzer Corridor'.

In order to hold the attention of the Allied armies, as this concentration of armoured strength raced across their rear, von Bock's Army Group B retained three Panzer

264. There were more than enough PzKpfw Is and IIs, 1,077 and 1,092 respectively being available to fill out the Panzer Regiments' strength. These shortages, plus supply and maintenance problems and last minute reshuffling of tanks, led to considerable changes in the actual composition of divisions. For example, 3rd Panzer went into battle with only 280 tanks: 109 PzKpfw Is (31 under establishment), 122 PzKpfw IIs (12 over) and 49 PzKpfw IIIs and IVs (15 under). 4th Panzer was better off with 340 tanks; 160 PzKpfw Is, 107 PzKpfw IIs, 41 PzKpfw IIIs and 32 PzKpfw IVs. According to its commander 7th Panzer Division also had some PzKpfw IIIs due to its more decisive role, although one wonders if the 'PzKpfw IIIs' of the Rommel Papers are not PzKpfw 38(t)s. The Germans could be very sensitive about using 'foreign' armour. The XIX Panzer Corps was well supplied with PzKpfw IIIs and IVs at the expense of divisions further north. The actual totals of vehicles which went into action on 10 May were 523 PzKpfw Is, 278 PzKpfw IVs, 955 PzKpfw IIs, 349 PzKpfw IIIs, 106 PzKpfw 35(t)s, 228 PzKpfw 38(t)s, 96 PzBefWg Is and 39 PzBefWg IIIs, a total of 2,439 battle tanks and 135 command vehicles.

Facing them was the largest tank force in the western world. Despite her industrial difficulties, France had constructed over 4,000 tanks in the previous decade and 3,254 were at the front, generally more heavily armed and armoured than their opponents. Nevertheless their design and deployment reflected a slow moving World War I concept of operations which Guderian intended to exploit. The French would be left permanently off balance and would be given no time to arrange deliberate counter-attacks. Their numerical superiority was, therefore, irrelevant, particularly as most of it was deployed in individual battalions in an infantry support role. Even though more concentrated armoured

units were available they lacked the Germans' experience and doctrine. A fast moving German armoured offensive striking as deeply as possible, as quickly as possible, relying on the confusion and inertia of its opponents to protect its exposed flanks had a high chance of success.

This was not consensus opinion in the conservatively minded High Command but, such was the amorphous way in which the German war was run, that *Panzergruppe* Kleist's instructions, once it had crossed the Meuse, were left vague and ill-defined. This was just what Guderian wanted.

A French Char B1 bis knocked out at Le Croisettes on the Somme. The turret and driver's vision slit bear marks from hits by an anti-tank gun. The Char B1 bis had a 75mm gun in the hull and a 47mm anti-tank gun in the turret. There were also two 7.5mm machine-guns.

A PzKpfw II Auf A SdKfz 121 crossing a pontoon bridge in France. This tank had a crew of three and was armed with one 2cm gun with 180 rounds and one machine-gun with 1,425 rounds. It was powered by an HL 62 TRM engine which developed 140 h.p. at 2,600 r.p.m. Added armour made its weight 9.5 tons, but it was capable of 40 k.p.h. and had a maximum range of 160 km.

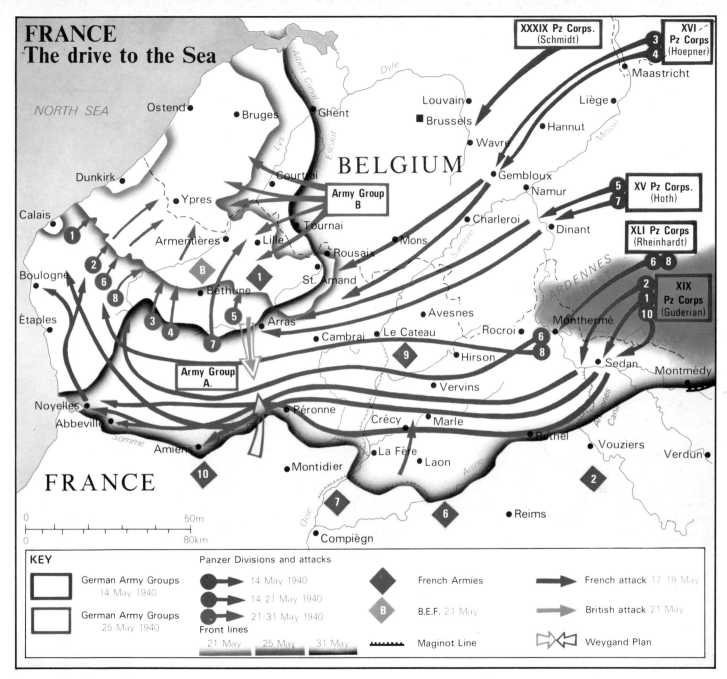

FRANCE
The drive to the Sea

NORTH SEA

BELGIUM

FRANCE

XXXIX Pz Corps. (Schmidt)

XVI Pz Corps (Hoepner)

XV Pz Corps. (Hoth)

XLI Pz Corps (Rheinhardt)

XIX Pz Corps (Guderian)

Army Group B

Army Group A.

ARDENNES FOREST

Ostend
Bruges
Ghent
Louvain
Brussels
Wavre
Hannut
Liège
Maastricht
Gembloux
Namur
Dunkirk
Ypres
Courtrai
Tournai
Charleroi
Dinant
Calais
Rousaix
Mons
Armentières
Lille
St. Amand
Monthermé
Boulogne
Béthune
Avesnes
Rocroi
Sedan
Montmédy
Étaples
Arras
Cambrai
Le Cateau
Hirson
Vouziers
Verdun
Noyelles
Péronne
Vervins
Rethel
Abbeville
Crécy
Marle
Amiens
La Fère
Laon
Montidier
Reims
Compiègn

ARDENNES Canal

Dyle
Escaut
Lys
Sambre
Meuse
Somme
Oise
Aisne

B

1

B

KEY

German Army Groups 14 May 1940	Panzer Divisions and attacks	
German Army Groups 25 May 1940	14 May 1940	French Armies
	14 21 May 1940	B.E.F. 21 May
	21 31 May 1940	

Front lines
21 May   25 May   31 May

French attack 17 19 May

British attack 21 May

Maginot Line

Weygand Plan

0   50m
0   80km

A mixed group of
38(t)s and PzKpfw
IIIs of the 25th
Panzer Regiment rest
prior to the attack on
the Somme crossing
areas in 1940.

Blitzkrieg Triumphant

During the early hours of 10 May the great offensive began. In the far north the bridge over
the Maas at Gannep fell into German hands
with the help of fifth columnists and 9th Panzer Division were soon across. The small and
weak Dutch Army offered little resistance and
the PzKpfw Is and IIs could come into their
own providing enough protection from an increasingly demoralised foe to be decisive.
Tilburg fell and the tanks achieved their first
objective as the Dutch withdrew northwards,
preventing a junction with the tanks of 1st
French Light Mechanised Division (D.L.M. –
Division Légère Méchanique) rushing up to
their relief. By 12 May, 9th Panzer with S.S.
motorised infantry had reached the major
bridge over the Maas at Moerdijk which had
been captured and held by German
parachutists. French attacks were beaten off
and XXXIX Corps moved on Rotterdam via
the bridge at Dordrecht, also captured by air-
borne units. The bombing of the city finally
cracked the Dutch resistance and on the 14th
the Netherlands surrendered, allowing 9th
Panzer Division to be redeployed to Antwerp.
A model campaign in the co-operation of air-
borne and mobile ground units had been
completed.

Further south it was the task of Army
Group B, led by XVI Panzer Corps, to hold
the attention of the Allied forces while the
decisive breakthrough occurred in the Ardennes. Only scattered resistance was met in

the 'Maastricht Appendix'. Dutch pill-boxes
were despatched with 75mm fire from PzKpfw
IVs. Anti-tank guns were outflanked and the
only serious difficulties were caused by mines.
Attempts to capture the bridges over the Maas
at Maastricht using German commandos
dressed in Dutch uniforms had failed but by
the end of 10 May pontoon crossings had been
built and the Corps was on its way to Belgium
over the Albert Canal bridges, successfully
secured by German glider troops.

The reconnaissance battalions' armoured

A Leichter
Panzerspähwagen
SdKfz 221 on the
Channel coast.
Lightly armoured,
these reconnaissance
vehicles had one
machine gun.

A PzBefWg III Auf E SdKfz 267 command tank in France. This tank was powered by a Maybach HL 108 TRM V-12 engine developing 300 h.p. at 3,000 r.p.m. and with armour ranging between 10mm and 30mm, and carried a dummy gun. In place of the main armament were extra radios for contacting H.Q. elements up to 40 km away. The tank had a five man crew and three machine-guns.

A PzKpfw II Auf a in France. This was one of the early marks which was distinguished by its unusual suspension. It was powered by a Maybach HL 51 TR petrol engine which developed 130 h.p. at 2,600 r.p.m. It had a maximum road speed of 40 k.p.h. and a road range of 210 km. Armament was one 2cm gun and a machine-gun with 180 and 1,425 rounds respectively.

A knocked out Char B1 bis. It appears to have suffered from an internal explosion since besides losing part of the engine deck cover and the right hand track, the commander's cupola has been blown off the turret and lies in front of the tank.

cars led the PzKpfw Is and IIs which in turn led the heavier PzKpfw IIIs and IVs. The following infantry and artillery were ready to converge on difficult opposition while the tanks withdrew to seek the easiest paths of advance. But few difficulties were faced as the Belgians retreated to join up with the French 1st Army. The Belgian units seemed to melt away as the tanks rushed forward. The further the tanks sped the greater the surprise of the defenders, who were shocked into surrender usually without a fight.

On the 12th, however, in the 'Gembloux Gap' between Huy and Tirlemont XVI Panzer Corps ran into more serious opposition; General Prioux's 1st French Cavalry Corps composed of the 2nd and 3rd D.L.M. Each division had 87 Somua S-35 mediums (47mm gun, 40-56mm armour), 87 Hotchkiss H-35 light battle tanks (37mm gun, 40-45mm armour and in 2nd's case 60 Renault A.M.R. light tanks (25mm gun or machine-gun, 13mm

armour). Their general superiority in armour and firepower, reinforced by some 20mm and 47mm armed Belgian tanks, helped in the opening skirmishes. However it soon became clear that German tactical control, both in terms of fire and manoeuvre, was more than a match for French technological superiority. The first isolated S-35s encountered were soon overwhelmed.

The battles increased in intensity on 13 May, a particularly heavy engagement developing around Orp le Grand between 4th Panzer and 3rd D.L.M. A large group of Somuas was spotted by the Division's reconnaissance aircraft and Stukas were called up to batter them. Long range fire fights developed, the German tanks moving from one position to another. Anti-tank guns were called in to protect exposed flanks and to support the tanks and to stop them expending too much ammunition. These long range encounters showed the inaccuracy of the French tank fire, for the over-worked commanders in their one man turrets were still recovering from the shock of the air attack. They also showed that most of the German weapons were ineffective against the French *Kolosse*. Strong French tank groups constituted a mobile threat which had to be destroyed. So with tank companies in *Breitkeil* (wide wedge) formation 5th Panzer Brigade charged forward to attack. This deployment allowed the tanks in the rear to support those at the point and contrasted with the looseness and dispersion on the French side. The German tanks zigzagged over the undulating countryside avoiding the desultory French fire and closing the range to make their own shells effective. The IVs' 75mm guns had the measure of the Somuas, but only at minimum range were the 37mm weapons of the IIIs effective. The PzKpfw IIs could only direct their 20mm fire at weak spots such as tracks and hatch hinges in the hope of inflicting at least some damage. More basic tactics were also used as the opposing vehicles circled round each other. One platoon commander, Lieutenant Wolters, had a lucky escape when a 47mm armour piercing shell penetrated the turret of his PzKpfw III. Charging up a hill under covering fire from the rest of his platoon the German tank rammed one of the Somuas tipping it down the slope and scaring the other two away.

The tank versus tank fighting remained very heavy as the French were pushed slowly westward. German tanks had their tracks shot off, or the turrets jammed by shell fire, but continued to fight. One PzKpfw II commander was killed when his periscope was shot away and he was forced to open the turret hatch to get his bearings in the swirling, dusty dogfight. Slowly the superior shooting, training, organisation and morale of the Germans began to tell. Swarms of German tanks were directed by radio onto single French vehicles. Surrounded by such packs the bewildered French commanders fired off the first shells which came to hand, even high explosive which were usually ineffective against the face hardened German armour. If it was bad for the Somuas it was even worse for the more weakly armed H-35s. Finally, attacked once more from the air, some crews surrendered while others retired. In the actions on 13 May, 3rd D.L.M. lost 30 Somuas and 70 H-35s. The 3rd D.L.M. claimed a rather inflated 164 Germans in return, but with possession of the field the mobile repair crews could get to work on damaged tanks and complete losses were relatively few.

This *Panzerschlacht bei Namur* achieved the aims of both sides. French 1st army was allowed to consolidate its Dyle position – as XVI Panzer Corps found to its cost the next day – and French attention was firmly riveted to the north, away from the mass of armour flowing into the Ardennes. With its way prepared by German agents XIX Panzer Corps

faced few problems in Luxembourg. When Belgium was reached the going became harder as 7th Panzer Division, leading XV Panzer Corps, had already found. The *Chasseurs Ardennais* had laid minefields, blown up bridges and barricaded roads, forcing the tanks to make time consuming diversions. In the

A German officer (right) interrogates two French soldiers captured during the fighting in 1940.

45

A PzKpfw 38(t) (3.7cm) TNHP-S on the French Channel coast. This tank taken over from the Czech Army was powered by a Skoda T-11 engine which developed 120 h.p. at 1,800 r.p.m. It had a maximum road speed of 40 k.p.h., a road range of 200 km and a cross country range of 115 km. Armament was one 37.2mm Skoda A3 gun and two machine-guns. Armour ranged from 8mm to 30mm.

A PzKpfw IV Auf D SdKfz 161 in France. Besides
an air identification flag on the rear deck, the tank
has petrol cans in a bracket on the side. It was
powered by a Maybach HL 108 TR which
developed 230 h.p. at 3,000 r.p.m. The tank had a
crew of five and an armament of one short
7.5cm KwK and two machine-guns. Armour was
between 8mm and 30mm.

German soldiers embark in a small rubber assault boat. It was in boats like this that the first infantry lodgement was made across the Meuse at Sedan.

narrow Ardennes roads traffic jams soon developed and there was some understandable confusion, with conflicting march routes for different divisions. Nevertheless, the advance continued with hard work by the military policemen and assault engineers assisted by some useful support from the Gross-Deutschland's *Sturmgeschütze*.

The French had sent forward Light Cavalry Divisions (D.L.C.) to screen their Meuse positions but these were soon outnumbered by the German armour. The particularly 'press-on' commander of 7th Panzer Division, General Erwin Rommel, found that in these battles of encounter, spraying fire in all direc-

tions could usually scatter the surprised and demoralised resistance from the tanks' path. The 37.2mm guns of his 38(t)s also had the measure of the H-35s and A.M.R.s (reconnaissance tanks). Further south, on 11 May, 30 tanks of 1st Panzer Division captured a whole battery of artillery. The German use of localised mass and mobile surprise was beginning to tell. By the 12th both Guderian and Rommel were on the Meuse, the latter reinforced by the 31st Panzer Regiment, half of 5th Panzer Division's 8th Panzer Brigade, left behind in the Ardennes crush.

The tanks could only fulfil supporting roles during the crossing of the river on 13 May as

fought back and no tanks could be ferried over. At Donchery 2nd Panzer, also delayed in the Ardennes, carried the eastern approaches to the river by a set-piece *Breitkeil* attack. Then the lighter tanks moved down to the water's edge, supported by the PzKpfw IVs in the rear. A fierce duel followed with the well camouflaged bunkers favourably situated on the other bank. The Germans shot off all their ammunition but got the first men across, to be followed later by tanks. Further south still, Guderian relied on massive air and artillery support for 1st and 10th Panzer, saving his tanks for the mobile phase to come.

By the next day pontoon bridges or ferries were getting the tanks across and Rommel was pushing ahead to Onhaye riding in a PzKpfw III. He had a narrow escape when the vehicles came under artillery and anti-tank fire and his tank slid off the road. The situation was only saved by the French shells setting off the smoke candles in the rear of the Regimental Commander's PzBefWg III. Stukas were called up to deal with the offending guns. At the major bridgehead 1st Panzer Brigade of 1st Panzer Division was being pushed across at Sedan as quickly as possible as the French counter-attacked with infantry supported by 37mm armed F.C.M. tanks. The commander of 1st Panzer Brigade was severely wounded when French tanks caught his vehicles, but anti-tank fire was able to hold them off long enough for the available PzKpfw IIIs and IVs to be thrown against them en masse. The French tanks were driven back, leaving more than half their number on the battlefield. The French infantry (with no anti-tank weapons) were soon dispersed and the position was secured. With 2nd Panzer now also across Guderian ordered them to strike westward, while 10th Panzer held the southern flank.

These crossings of the Meuse and Rommel's lunge forward unnerved General Corap, the commander of the French 9th Army. In

Left: A PzKpfw IV on the Aisne in 1940. It is shooting at French troops in the woods in the background.

the emphasis was firmly on infantry and, as usual, the engineers. The Germans had no specialised amphibious tanks and fire support was the usual armoured task. At Dinant the crossing was stalled by defenders until they were 'shot in' by PzKpfw IVs and IIs driving along the river bank. French pill-boxes with unarmoured embrasures were all too vulnerable to tank fire. Up-river 6th Panzer finally arrived in eastern Monthermé to face heavy fire from the defenders on the far bank. Again tanks were called in and the slow reduction of the defences began. The most important French bunker under the hotel by the bridge was thus destroyed but the French

A captured French Hotchkiss H39 tank. It was armed with a long 37mm gun and a co-axial machine gun. The flag would have been one of those carried for signalling since these tanks had no radio.

the early hours of 15 May he ordered withdrawal to new defences. This was fatal. Having once allowed the Panzers to gain momentum they would be on any future 'defensive line' before the slow moving and slower thinking French could build it. The 1st Panzer Division still faced some serious resistance to be broken by its infantry but 2nd was now able to push ahead.

A French motorised column, probably one of the advanced units of 2nd Reserve Armoured Division (D.C.R.) was surprised in Paunois sur Vence by a leading German tank column led by a PzKpfw III. The Germans scattered the crews and shot up the vehicles with machine-gun and high explosive gunfire. The Hotchkiss H-39 tanks (Renaults to the Germans) also proved remarkably vulnerable to accurate 37mm tank fire, even at ranges of 400 metres. Five tanks encountered were soon in flames and 15 more were claimed in another battle in Jandun, the next village. The inaccuracy of the surprised French crews saved the Germans.

As the German Panzers pressed forward, away from the rest of the German Army, they needed to conserve ammunition as supply became more of a problem. Ammunition and fuel kept moving up the undefended roads but the situation was potentially very dangerous. Safety was in movement and, ignoring the threat to the flanks, the tanks kept going even when gearbox oil and radiator water ran low. This 'press-on' spirit could backfire, as when one of 2nd Panzer's PzKpfw IVs was blown up as it passed over a bridge at the head of the advance, but even this caused only a minor delay.

The tanks of 6th Panzer now managed to cross at Monthermé after considerable fighting. They surged forward through the disintegrating 9th Army, past abandoned guns and surrendering men. Little resistance was offered. Four tanks caught 115 French transport vehicles in two groups on one road and drove up and down alongside shooting them up. The new found reliability and ease of driving of the PzKpfw 35(t) was coming into its own. The Division then met more confused elements of 2nd D.C.R. and completed the process of cutting off most of the tanks in the north from their infantry and supplies in the south. The 35(t)s soon scared away even the French division's heavy Chars B. By the end of the day Montcornet had been captured, an advance of 37 miles from Monthermé.

These French D.C.R.s provided the major forces which the French Army could throw against the vulnerable flanks of the 'Panzer Corridor' that were fast developing. Yet they suffered from the German's superior speed of operation as much as any other French unit.

On the same day that 2nd D.C.R. was cut in half, 1st D.C.R. was caught near Flavion in the act of refuelling by 7th Panzer, as usual pressing westwards as fast as possible. The very powerful, but immobile, Chars B were set on fire to avoid capture. Those that did fight back had their tracks shot off by the 37.2mm guns of the PzKpfw 38(t)s, preventing the traversing of the fixed main armament. The 25th Panzer Regiment swung round the opposition in best Panzer style. Then the 31st Panzer Regiment of 5th Panzer Division coming up in 7th's wake, got to work on the Chars B, concentrating their fire on weak spots, such as the gun mountings, of these 60mm armoured monsters. The Bs could use their 47mm and 75mm guns to knock out any German tank but, as usual, tactics, training and *Angriffsgeist* (attacking spirit) told, and the French withdrew beaten. The 7th Armoured, meanwhile, were finding Stuka bomb craters as much of a problem as the French and by the end of the day were 17 miles from the starting point at Cerfontaine, a slightly disappointing advance by its own standards.

On 16 May greater progress was made. The 1st and 2nd Panzer Divisions met with 6th at Montcornet and, on his own initiative, Guderian set informal divisional boundaries for the further advance. Kleist had been left behind by the speed of this headlong armoured advance and was becoming increasingly reluctant to sanction further advances. By the end of the day, however, 1st and 2nd Panzer had advanced 40 miles, often through almost deserted countryside. The 2nd Panzer Division met the rested 3rd D.L.C. near Montcornet and once more, as in the Ardennes, its dispersed H-35s fell back. Advanced units of 6th Panzer were in Guise and 8th Panzer Division, who had faced the most difficult crossing of the Meuse, was finally across and catching up.

It was Hoth's XV Panzer Corps, however,

that made the greatest individual gains that day. Rommel's 7th Panzer ran into the fortifications built by the French along the border and their 25mm and 47mm anti-tank fire proved uncomfortably effective against the German tanks. An anti-tank ditch made the road the only possible axis of advance but this was blocked by obstacles. Tanks and artillery opened fire in the fading light as engineers moved up under smoke cover to blow the obstacle. The tanks pressed through as fast as they could, firing in all directions and kept going through the night to maximise surprise. In Avesnes a few Chars B, relics of 1st D.C.R., overcame their shock to destroy some German tanks but the Bs were eventually finished off by the PzKpfw IV of Lieutenant Hanke, Rommel's aide-de-camp. With no orders from Hoth, Rommel pushed ahead to Landrecies and the Sambre, by now conserving his limited supplies of ammunition. By this time the tank commanders were able to order French troops to throw away their weapons without having to fire a shot. At Landrecies the bridge was taken intact and

A PzBefWg III Ausf E leading a company of PzKpfw II tanks. The tank was equipped with three machine-guns but had a wooden dummy in place of the main armament.

Hanke's PzKpfw IV drove into the courtyard of the barracks on the far side where he ordered the French officers to march their men into captivity. By 05.15 on 17 May Rommel's two leading tank battalions were at Le Cateau, 50 miles from their previous day's starting point.

Now, however, the rest of the division had to catch up and, leaving his tanks in the normal defensive 'hedgehog' formation, Rommel drove back in his half-track escorted by a PzKpfw III. The pace was beginning to tell and the III broke down but a PzKpfw IV that had already fallen by the wayside and been repaired by its crew was commandeered in its stead. Despite some difficult moments French demoralisation remained almost complete and the division was re-assembled although there were still vulnerable gaps between units. For the loss of 35 killed and 59 wounded, 7th Panzer Division had taken 100,000 prisoners and 100 tanks. Even more important, a bridgehead had been established over the main line the French had planned to hold.

Further south 6th and 1st Panzer Divisions managed to lodge similar bridgeheads on the Sambre-Oise canal during the 17th. The 8th Panzer Division was also bringing its 38(t)s

into action along the Oise. Now, however, Hitler and the High Command became concerned about the extended nature of the armoured penetrations. The tanks were ordered to stop, and the advance ground to a halt. While argument raged between the higher commanders, the crews took a well earned rest. They replaced engine parts worn out by nearly 70 miles continuous running, lubricated bearings and replenished with supplies from columns that had caught up with the tanks. This work was almost interrupted when 1st Panzer was attacked by the unsupported tanks of De Gaulle's 4th D.C.R., but

A PzKpfw IV Ausf D in France. The Ausf A and D had a stepped frontal plate with the driver's vision port forward of the hull machine gun.

One of the few Char FCM36 tanks in service with the French in 1940 after it was knocked out on the Aisne. The tank carried a 37mm gun with a co-axial machine gun.

these were eventually driven off by tanks straight from field workshops and PzKpfw I based 47mm tank destroyers. To protect against further similar thrusts, 10th Panzer moved up from the southern edge of the break-out area on the Meuse where it had been guarding against counter-attacks.

Guderian eventually received permission for a 'reconnaissance in force' which he interpreted as re-opening the attack at full strength. The 2nd Panzer Division after thrusting aside some Chars B of 2nd D.C.R. made the crossing of the canal. More Chars B were thrown against 6th Panzer's bridgeheads and as usual the 37.2mm guns of the 35(t)s were ineffective. Only shots in the tracks immobilised the French tanks and 88mm A.A. guns were the only effective protection.

On 18 May the 'reconnaissance' swept on and 1st Panzer advanced 30 miles to the River

Somme before the morning was over. Further north 6th Panzer ran into more trouble with Chars B, but 2nd D.C.R. was now running out of tanks and after a two hour battle the remaining *Kolosse* were overwhelmed. By evening the 35(t)s were south of Cambrai. Rommel also had problems with French armour when 1st D.L.M., redeployed from the north, drove against the scattered elements of his division. The German guns again proved ineffective against the Somuas and the remaining tank battalion had great difficulty in fighting its way round to its companions at Le Cateau. The fuel and ammunition supplies were left behind but Rommel decided to drive on to Cambrai with a motorised rifle battalion supported by those few tanks with enough fuel and some 20mm guns on half-tracks. Spreading as much fire and dust as they could, the Germans convinced the French that a major tank attack was on its way and the town fell to Rommel's bluff.

Things were not quite so easy in the north where 5th Panzer was having a hard time from the 1st D.L.M. and 1st North African Division in the Forest of Mormal after capturing Maubeuge. In front of the Sambre resistance had been weak and the tank crews drove with open hatches as they shot up villages and scattered the defenders. Now, however, with a forest filled with enemy strongpoints, minefields, infantry, artillery and tanks, the German tanks found the going harder. Mainly infantry and artillery had to be used to dislodge the defence but where they could, the Division's various tank types deployed into *Breitkeil* as Somuas sallied forth in more open areas to attack. The offensive slowly made progress, the tanks withdrew to replenish with ammunition before pressing on accompanied by infantry and engineers supported by heavy artillery fire. Infantrymen had to be warned from riding on the tanks because they drew fire. As more French tanks appeared the emphasis swung to anti-tank guns, supported by Stukas. Tanks could not win all battles even in this campaign. However, by the next day, as the French were held in combat by less mobile elements of the division, the tanks pushed on towards Solesmes.

The 19th saw the German armour crossing the old Somme battlefield, now 'officially' advancing once more to gain a bridgehead over the Somme. The 10th Panzer Division, repulsed at Ham, was left to guard against a further attack by De Gaulle's mixed force of Chars B, and D2, Somuas and Renault R-35s. Stukas and anti-tank guns rather than tanks were again the main weapons used to stop the French tanks. The French attack did not worry the Germans unduly but the need to give the worn out men and machines of the Panzer Divisions some time for rest and repair forced

Panzergruppe Kleist to stop before the Somme or Canal du Nord were crossed. Following the withdrawal of the Allied Armies in the north, XVI Panzer Corps, after resting near Charleroi, was by then coming down from the north, pressing back French 1st Army towards Valenciennes.

A Renault BS tank parked in the entrance to the citadel of Belfort. This tank was originally built in 1916 and armed with a machine gun.

A PzKpfw II crossing a pontoon bridge over a canal in France. The tank commander who wears awards from the Polish campaign has an infantry style grey cap which was a temporary measure before black caps were introduced in place of berets.

Rommel had spent 19 May resting his division but at 01.40 on the 20th he was again on the move, with his tanks reaching south of Arras by 06.00 but again creating difficulties by outrunning their support. Guderian began slightly later with 1st Panzer, moving on Amiens. Resistance was virtually nil in the excellent tank country of the Picardy Plain and by 08.45 the city was reached. On the way a British fighter airfield was over-run as the Hurricanes took off to escape. The 1st Panzer Brigade moved into the city and destroyed the British battalion holding it. Meanwhile, 2nd Panzer took a British gun battery at Albert with only training ammunition. They had not been expecting the Germans so soon. These German tanks were in Abbeville by 19.00 and one tank battalion actually reached the sea at Noyelles. The 'Panzer Corridor' was complete but the morale of the British forces who were now being encountered had not yet cracked

like that of their allies. The 6th Panzer's 35(t)s had a hard time at Doullens against a British Territorial Brigade which used its anti-tank weapons to good effect. Leaving the British to be destroyed by less mobile forces the tanks swept round to the north.

The British made more serious difficulties on 21 May. As Rommel's tanks moved to outflank Arras to the west there was near panic when they were struck by 64 heavily armoured British Matilda Infantry Tanks. They seemed impervious to German fire and were able to destroy those German tanks they met. PzKpfw 38(t)s were despatched by 0.5inch machine-gun fire from the small Mark I infantry tanks, while PzKpfw IIIs could be easily penetrated by the Mark II's 2-pounder (40mm) weapons. These guns could fire shells right through the German tanks. The 25th Panzer Regiment, returning to counter-attack, ran into well emplaced British 2-pounder anti-tank guns supported by some Somuas from the remnants of 3rd D.L.M. They lost three PzKpfw IVs, six PzKpfw IIIs and 'a number' of light tanks. Heavy German artillery and A.A. fire eventually stopped the British attack which was limited in both capability and scope, but it was a severe shock to the Germans at all levels, including the highest. The XLI Panzer Corps was diverted to Rommel's support and 10th Panzer Division was taken from Guderian and put into *Panzergruppe* reserve to guard against similar incidents.

The commander of XIX Panzer Corps spent this eventful day fretting and awaiting new orders while his crews worked on their tanks. On 22 May, however, the advance began again with the target now the Channel ports. The 2nd Panzer Division advanced on Boulogne and 1st on Calais. They left some forces behind to guard the Somme bridges for not even the motorised infantry had caught up. The 10th Panzer Division was intended for Dunkerque but was unavailable due to its redeployment. By then there was little air support and more British aerial activity. Opposition was also becoming stiffer on the ground. Point companies of PzKpfw IIIs and IVs were at first able to deal with the individual French guns they encountered. One lead PzKpfw III, under Lieutenant Behr, was able to knock out two 47mm anti-tank guns and a 75mm howitzer encountered in one village with accurate high explosive fire. Gear box trouble delayed Behr's tank and the lead was taken over by 'Jochen II' which soon dealt with a 25mm anti-tank gun. Serious opposition was experienced in Samer, however, and in the confined conditions of the town Behr's tank and 'Jochen II' were knocked out in respective duels with a 75mm gun and an anti-tank gun. Only after the complete deployment of the other companies of the battalion was the French position worn down. At least one more tank was lost in the out-

skirts of Boulogne itself, which was strongly held by five naval coast defence forts, a motley collection of French troops and two British Guards Battalions sea-lifted in that day.

During the night the German tanks reconnoitred round the town. One crew of a PzKpfw IV company directed to reconnoitre the large Fort de la Crèche guarding the northern approaches to the town used their tank as an unmanned 'mine detector', sending it slowly over a suspected bridge and then jumping back in. The defenders of the fort came out to meet the Germans convinced that they could not be the enemy but dashed back when they recognised their mistake. The major assault was fixed for 23 May and around Boulogne tank repair crews worked feverishly to repair the previous day's casualties, welding closed the holes and repairing damaged components.

The first targets were the forts. Under fire from British and French destroyers, the attack on Fort de la Crèche went in behind a smoke

An A13 Cruiser of the 10th Hussars after it was knocked out by German anti-tank guns during fighting near Huppy on 27 May 1940. This tank was capable of speeds up to 50 k.p.h. though its engine could be temperamental.

A mixed German column on the Aisne. Besides a PzKpfw I and other light tanks there is a Horch Kfz 4 × 4 medium car.

screen. Two companies of PzKpfw IIIs and IVs were used, each accompanied by a dismounted motor-cycle company, being allowed this time to ride into action on the tanks. The tank guns were slowly able to knock out the fort's gun positions allowing the assault infantry to capture it. As they moved on the town two tanks were knocked out by a troop of British 3.7 inch A.A. guns, one of the first uses of this powerful weapon in an anti-tank role. At another fort the effect of the tanks was more direct as they crashed through the gate of the outer wall and blazed away in all directions, their way blocked by a barrier of burning vehicles. The fire of the surprised defenders slackened and one tank commander, Lieutenant Hoffmann, seized the national flag carried for air identification purposes and ran it up the fort's mast. He was wounded but the demoralised French defenders, 300 strong, decided to give themselves up even though their guns were still intact. Even against fortifications the power of the Panzers to shock their opponents into surrender was decisive.

All the forts were eventually taken, but the British defenders of the town itself, now reinforced by Royal Marines and naval personnel, proved harder to dislodge. Under cover of heavy artillery the light tank companies supported by mediums, approached the citadel only to find that every building was defended. The tanks withdrew and then attacked again, with close infantry support, trying to find an easier axis of advance. Fire from PzKpfw IVs and the division's company of PzKpfw I based self-propelled 150mm infantry guns slowly demolished the houses over the heads of the defenders. Road barriers could be crushed but the old citadel walls proved more difficult. Despite air attacks by the Luftwaffe, fighting continued into the night. Most of the British troops were evacuated but the defenders held out throughout the following day. German tanks placed themselves in a position from which they could fire into the harbour and duels ensued with Allied destroyers. Some casualties were inflicted on the British ships, and tank fire may have played a part in sinking the large French destroyer *Chacal* on the 24th.

It was not until 25 May that the town surrendered under the threat of heavier air bombardment.

This diversion, and that at Calais, were delaying the main aim of completing the isolation of the B.E.F. and its French allies from any chance of evacuation. Guderian was anxious to capture Dunkerque. The 1st Panzer Division driving off an armoured break-out from Calais by British Light and Cruiser tanks from 3rd R.T.R. finally began to advance on the 23rd, 10th Panzer being given the role of reducing Calais. The desperate British and French rearguards stopped 1st Panzer on the Aa Canal, but the armoured pressure was increasing on the Allies. The XLI Panzer Corps then came up alongside 1st Panzer at St Omer. The XXXIX Panzer Corps had by then outflanked Arras and XVI Panzer Corps was brought round from the north to close the gap between these divisions and XLI Corps. It looked as if a massed armoured attack was about to win a final decisive victory. On the 24th, 1st Panzer seized bridgeheads over the Canal and Guderian ordered as many tanks as possible of 2nd Panzer to disentangle themselves from Boulogne for support. The 10th Panzer Division, who lost half their tanks that day against stubborn resistance in Calais, were ordered to conserve their armour for the final offensive next day.

However, on 24 May came the order to halt. Hitler, goaded by Rundstedt, was disturbed by the British success at Arras and wished to save his tanks from the easily defended, marshy Dunkerque countryside criss-crossed by water courses for the final defeat of France. There were reports of 50 per cent tank unserviceability which, though true for brief periods, underestimated the capacity of the mobile tank repair teams. Nevertheless, the bridgehead over the Aa Canal was to be abandoned and Dunkerque left to the infantry and Luftwaffe. The ever insubordinate

Guderian did feel justified in using 2nd Panzer's tanks to help the Gross-Deutschland and the S.S. *Leibstandarte*, now under his Corps command, to 'secure' positions over the Aa but after that the German tanks were stopped along the entire front. The 3rd Panzer Regiment of 2nd Panzer Division had to content themselves with rescuing Sepp Dietrich, commander of the *Leibstandarte*, from a party of outflanked British soldiers who had ambushed his command car. The 10th Panzer Division also continued their pressure on Calais. They refused air support since they would need to withdraw and Lieutenant-General Schaal doubted the effectiveness of air bombardment against the fortifications. Combined tank and infantry assaults finally obtained the surrender of the garrison on 26 May.

The British were given their chance to solidify their rearguard, being safe from further armoured shocks until the evening of the

A German soldier examines a knocked out Hotchkiss H39. The 37mm gun appears to have been hit, the tank has shed a track and sustained other damage to the hull.

A German motor-cyclist looks at the battered remains of a PzKpfw II in northern France. Hits have been scored on the armour around the driver's vision slit, and the turret and part of the right side of the tank have been blown off.

26th when the rested Panzer Divisions were once again let loose. With his Corps further reinforced, Guderian pushed his tanks and motorised infantry on Dunkerque. The 1st Panzer Division was on the left with 4th Panzer Brigade of 10th Panzer Division ordered to support the Gross-Deutschland and tanks of 2nd Panzer providing similar support for the *Leibstandarte* in the direction of Wormhoudt, south of Dunkerque. The conditions put a premium on close infantry/tank co-operation. Where they could move freely, mixed groups of the latter's PzKpfw IIs and IVs pushed on, dealing with artillery observers in water towers with 75mm fire and British armoured cars with bursts of five shots from 20mm KwK. The fire of 20mm and machine-guns was able, for a time, to deal with anti-tank guns and the difficult country proved the greatest problem. Tanks were able to help others which slid off the road into the ditches. Eventually, however, resistance became severe and it was not until 28 May that Wormhoudt was captured.

Further east there had been hard fighting on XV Panzer Corps' front as the Germans tried to cut off those French forces fighting in the Lille area. Problems were encountered in building a sufficiently strong bridge across the La Bassée Canal, blocked by sunken barges and under the fire of some very troublesome

A German soldier loads his MG34 machine gun as the crew go into action during a river crossing operation in France. The MG34 is on its sustained fire tripod.

British troops. Shells from a PzKpfw IV were needed to eliminate the British snipers who were delaying the engineers. With his infantry bridgeheads under attack from some of the 16 remaining British Matildas a PzKpfw III was rushed across to the first rickety pontoons to give protection. A PzKpfw IV, manned by Rommel himself, also engaged from the other side of the river. It halted the leading British tank, probably by blowing off a Mark I's exposed tracks. The PzKpfw III's fire and, more importantly, that of a 105mm field howitzer also helped in stopping the British attack. The 25th Panzer Regiment were then sent across, reinforced by 5th Panzer Brigade

put under Rommel's command. The advance was slow against heavy resistance including tanks. The 25th Panzer Regiment driving through the night reached Lomme, west of Lille, where they deployed into defensive positions soon to be reinforced by the rest of the Division. The trap finally closed and 35,000 French troops surrendered.

By that time the tanks had been finally withdrawn to prepare for the attack in the south, a very necessary precaution. The 7th Panzer Divison had only 86 tanks fit for operations, only five of which were the vital PzKpfw IVs. The Panzers' success however had been almost complete. *Sichelschnitt* had

61

French prisoners-of-war line up to be searched by the Germans.

worked out as well as any of its planners might have hoped. The tanks had used their sheer mobility to dumbfound the Allied Command and cut their forces in two. Stopping them allowed the Allies to evacuate many of their men from Dunkerque which held out against the German infantry until 4 June. These Allied forces had however lost all their heavy equipment and their military capacity was, for the moment, negligible. Belgium and Holland had been taken. It only remained to finish off France using the same techniques of armoured mobility which had won the decisive battle.

Fall Rot a postscript

The final conquest of France, *Fall Rot* (Case Red), began on 5 June with the German tanks redeployed to lead the advance south from the southern perimeter of the 'Panzer Corridor'. Army Group B striking first on the right had XV Panzer Corps under Hoth. The Corps contained 7th and 5th Panzer Divisions deployed along the lower Somme. Further east and also subordinate to Army Group B was *Panzergruppe* Kleist with von Wietersheim's XIV Panzer Corps around Amiens, composed of 10th and 9th Panzer Divisions (the latter having held the Somme bridgeheads while the others were fighting to the north) and with Hopner's XVI Panzer Corps with 3rd and 4th Panzer around Péronne. Army Group A had a second such group, *Panzergruppe* Guderian, his achievement having been acknowledged by this increase in status. He commanded Schmidt's XXXIX Panzer Corps with 1st and 2nd Panzer Divisions and Reinhardt's XLI with 6th and 8th. Each Panzer Corps had at least an Army or S.S. motorised infantry division under command to help prevent too great an outrunning of support. There was some limited armoured re-equipment with some new 50mm armed PzKpfw IIIs coming into service to assist against Chars B and Somuas and three more *Sturmgeschütz* batteries for the infantry.

Opposition to the offensive was at first severe. The French now recognised the

weakness of the Germans and with 75mm guns and 47mm anti-tank guns in their anti-tank defences of the 'Weygand Line' refought Kleist's Panzers to a standstill, proving that armour was not sufficient against a stubborn foe. The German tanks were able to advance only a few miles from their bridgeheads. Rommel had still to cross the river. Under cover of artillery fire two bridges over the river, one rail and one road, fell to 7th Panzer's infantry and the rails were torn up to allow the tanks to cross. There was a delay

A knocked out French Somua S35 tank. The crew have escaped through the side hatch. This tank had a powerful 47mm gun, good armour and a top speed of 40 k.p.h. and in its time was regarded as the best tank in the world.

63

when a PzKpfw IV shed its track on the western entrance to the railway bridge and dug itself in with torn up sleepers jamming in the road wheels. A half hour was wasted as the tank was pushed and pulled over by a 38(t) and another IV. A tank battalion was sent up the river against Hengest to 'soften up' the French position which was holding up pontoon bridge building operations. More delay occurred when the tanks stuck fast as they turned off up a steep hill and the crews came under heavy machine-gun fire when they dismounted to extricate themselves. The division's self-propelled 150mm gun company was brought up to give covering fire and a motor cycle battalion eventually saved the situation. At 16.00 the major attack started with 25th Panzer Regiment in the lead, supported by all the other arms of the division. A heavy fire was laid down and the Germans eventually broke through the hard fighting French African troops. The Chateau de Quesnoy had been converted into a fortress with loopholes cut into its outer wall and PzKpfw IVs again came into their own with their 75mm shells. In best *Blitzkrieg* style Le Quesnoy was bypassed and the tanks pressed on destroying concentrations of French troops as they were passed, the rest of the division following in the tanks' wake. By evening, however, only 8 miles had been covered and counter-attacks led by tanks came in throughout the night, the German armour making some contribution to their repulse.

On 6 June Kleist remained stalled with up to 65 tank casualties and again 7th Panzer took the lead, advancing over 12 miles. On the 7th he advanced another 30 miles towards Rouen using the tracked mobility of his tanks to strike across country like a tide ebbing round the blocked villages and major roads. The tracked tanks made paths for the wheeled support vehicles to follow, overcoming the deficiencies in the mobility of the support vehicles. With the whole conceptual basis of their defence shattered, the French abandoned their positions and only isolated resistance was encountered, which could be crushed by the German tanks. One tank company was specifically ordered to cut the Paris – Dieppe road at Saumont. After taking an ammunition depot, the commander, Captain Schutz, accomplished his mission and captured several surprised French vehicles as they came along the road.

On 8 June, 7th Panzer advanced on Rouen hoping to divert at the last minute and capture by surprise the Seine bridges at Elbeuf, south of the city. The division moved on, all elements again in mutual support. The bridge over the Andrelle was blown and the tanks began to ford, but a PzKpfw II went beyond its wading depth blocking the passage. Parts of the blown up bridge and riverside willows were used to raise the height of the river bed, and a PzKpfw III which had already crossed towed the II out. Again villages were bypassed by the leading tanks but some British rearguards delayed the advance of the rear echelons and Rommel was not able to mount an artillery barrage to feign an attack on Rouen. When these units eventually came up, Rommel despatched his tanks down to the bridges. Interestingly, Rommel in his command half-track did not have the correct radio to communicate directly with the tanks. Long range communication had also failed in the night conditions. Mistaken as British Allies by the surprised locals the tanks passed unmanned enemy guns. The Panzer Regiment eventually halted and, escorted by five PzKpfw IIIs, the Motor-cycle Battalion was sent up to capture the bridges. Due to the delays in Elbeuf the bridges had been blown. Even Rommel could not win every time. Isolated and not knowing where the rest of 7th Panzer was Rommel prudently withdrew.

Rouen had fallen to 5th Panzer, advancing

on Rommel's right. The few French defenders hoped to engage the Germans down the long, straight roads of the city, so keeping them away from the river. The German tanks however drove down the lateral roads, firing at intersections and working their way up undefended streets protected by buildings at each end. Eventually they reached the river but again the bridges were blown.

On 9 June, Army Group A finally struck

Left; A Leichter Panzerspähwagen SdKfz 221 The grills covered the open turret and were for protection against hand grenades. *Above:* Rouen in flames. Two Germans sit on an elderly Renault tank.

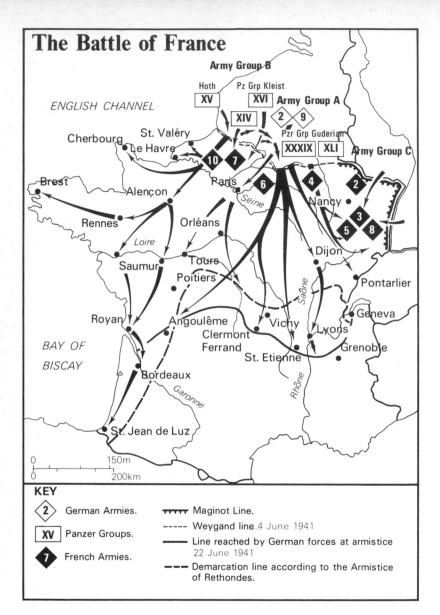

The Battle of France

ENGLISH CHANNEL

Army Group B

Hoth   Pz Grp Kleist
XV   XVI   Army Group A

XIV   2 | 9

Pzr Grp Guderian
XXXIX | XLI   Army Group C

Cherbourg
St. Valéry
Le Havre

Brest

Alençon
Paris
Seine
10 | 7
6   4   2
Nancy
3
5 | 8

Rennes

Orléans

Loire

Saumur
Tours
Poitiers

Dijon

Saône

Pontarlier

Royan
Angoulême
Vichy
Lyons
Geneva

BAY OF
BISCAY

Clermont
Ferrand
St. Etienne
Grenoble

Bordeaux
Garonne

Rhône

St. Jean de Luz

0   150m
0   200km

KEY

2 — German Armies.

XV — Panzer Groups.

7 — French Armies.

⊤⊤⊤⊤ Maginot Line.

----- Weygand line 4 June 1941

——— Line reached by German forces at armistice
22 June 1941

- - - Demarcation line according to the Armistice
of Rethondes.

with infantry intended to make the first breakthrough over the Aisne for the tanks to follow. Again resistance was heavy and only one small bridgehead was obtained, but Guderian soon had 1st and 2nd Panzer Divisions across. At 6.30 on the 10th the *Panzerangriff* began with tanks and infantry in close co-operation. Again the French fought hard using woods and villages as the basis of their 'hedgehogs' and these were left to the infantry while the tanks pressed on across country. Long tank battles against Chars B of the 3rd D.C.R. were decided in the Germans' favour with the latter's tactics and, possibly, some 50mm PzKpfw IIIs helping tip the scales 1st Panzer would have had first call on these vehicles. Nevertheless heavy tank casualties were suffered.

Co-ordinated tank and infantry attacks by XXXIX Corps continued on 11 and 12 June. The 'Weygand Line' was eventually broken and as French resistance finally weakened the pace quickened. Contradictory orders were then coming in, but Guderian kept on to the south, supported by equally 'press on' subordinates. St Dizier fell on the 14th, Langres on the 15th and Besancon on the 16th as the French will to resist finally cracked and the advance became virtually a route march. With motorised infantry on the Swiss border on the 17th, Guderian, anticipating superior orders, turned east to take the Maginot Line in the rear. Around midnight on the 17th, 1st Panzer Division signalled Guderian that it had reached its corps objective but the tanks and supply vehicles still had fuel to go on. Guderian gave the order and Belfort was captured, its fortress finally fell to guns and infantry on 18 June. The 2nd, 6th and 8th Panzer Divisions did the same up the line of fortresses to the north. Two days later the armistice negotiations began.

Kleist had moved eastwards to exploit Guderian's break through, crossing the Marne at Chateau Thierry on the 12th. By the Armistice 3rd Panzer was almost at Grenoble in the Alps with 4th Panzer also past Lyons on its right. Kleist had 10th Panzer at Mâcon and 9th at Clermont Ferrand. Nothing, it appeared, could stand in the way of the German tanks.

What, however, of Rommel whom we left on 9 June as Guderian's offensive began? Together with 5th Panzer Division he was ordered to strike towards Le Havre to cut off Allied forces retreating to the sea. He advanced at high speed, his tanks sometimes on the road, sometimes off it in suitable going. Enemy forces were quickly dispersed by fire in the usual manner and a delighted division reached the sea between St Valéry and Fécamp. Rothenburg's PzBefWg III crashed through the sea wall down to the water's edge in the celebration. Two tank companies helped Rommel push at top speed to St Leonard, preventing any enemy break-out to the south of St Valéry and the roads were blocked by six of the tanks. The rest of the companies' tanks were ordered to rejoin the regiment but, due to a traffic jam with the relieving motor-cyclists, only one company could accompany Rommel back. On the return journey an anti-tank gun then opened up hitting the track of the lead tank, which was abandoned by its crew. The other tanks seemed shocked into inactivity but under fire Rommel berated the commander for his lack of aggressiveness and ordered one of the other tanks, a PzKpfw II, to open fire. Bursts of 20mm and machine-gun tracer soon scared off the isolated anti-tank gun.

Advancing on St Valéry on 11 June, the 25th Panzer Regiment was able to push through British defences to bombard the harbour. Calls to surrender were unheeded and Rommel then opened fire with his surrounding tanks until less mobile weapons could be brought up. Shells from a PzKpfw IV succeeded in smashing down the defences on the harbour mole. Next day the Panzer Regiment was kept by Rommel as a mobile reserve and they were eventually used to roll into the town against the defenders, mainly men of the 51st Highland Division, who were demoralised by the bombardment and surrendered. Some

German soldiers ferry a motor-cycle across a canal on a pneumatic assault boat.

12,000 men, of whom 8,000 were British, were carried off into captivity by 7th Panzer Division. Le Havre was occupied on 14 June.

The 7th Panzer Division was next launched on Cherbourg, while 5th Panzer was directed to Rennes and Brest. The advance was resumed on the 17th against French troops who, with the knowledge that an armistice had already been asked for, had no further wish to fight. Only pausing to refuel, Rommel's leading reconnaissance battalion covered 150 miles in a single day, leaving most of the tanks behind. Eventually these were brought up to attack through the night on the 18th to take the dominating hills west of Cherbourg. Opposition was again weak, despite difficult bocage terrain, and Cherbourg was bombarded into surrender on the 19th. During the entire campaign 7th Panzer had taken almost 100,000 prisoners, 341 guns and 458 A.F.V.s for the cost of 682 killed and 1,942 wounded or missing.

So the activities of the German tanks ended with massive demonstrations of mobility against a disintegrated foe. It had always been this aspect of the German tanks which had been decisive. With leaders at all levels trained to think and act fast, speed and skill of manoeuvre had compensated for deficiencies in armour and firepower. The tank based Panzer Division was an instrument to which conventional military wisdom had yet to find an answer and Hitler's *Blitzkrieg* strategy had been triumphantly vindicated. Now the way was clear for the German tanks to gain the *Lebensraum* (living space) in Eastern Europe that was the centrepiece of Nazi foreign policy. Mechanical speed would surely conquer distance against the hordes of *Untermensch* (sub-humans). There were few question marks in the confident minds of the *Panzerwaffe* as it began re-organisation for its greatest test.

German Tanks 1939-1940

PzKpfw I (SdKfz 101)

This was the first *Landwirtschaftschlepper* (Agricultural Tractor) designed to provide an easily available training vehicle for the new Panzer Divisions. A specification was issued in 1932 and the Krupp design chosen. Mass production of the chassis began in 1934 and continued until 1941, although the last were used for specialised purposes. Few, if any, PzKpfw I battle tanks were completed after 1938. There were two models.

Ausf A the initial production order with trailing rear idler and 57 h.p. (German rating) Krupp M305 petrol engine. Details were: weight 5.4 tonnes, road speed 37 k.p.h., road range 145 km, cross country range 97 km.

Ausf B experience showed that these early tanks were underpowered and the design was revised with a 100 h.p. Maybach NL38TR power unit. This necessitated lengthening the hull and suspension. Weight was now 6 tonnes, road range 140 km and cross country range 115 km.

Both types had all round armour protection of 13mm and were armed with two 7.92mm MG13 machine-guns in a small turret offset to the right. The crew was two. The builders were Henschel, Wegman, MAN and, for later chassis, Böhmisch Mahrische Mäschinenfabrik (ex CKD/Praga).

PzKpfw II (SdKfz 121)

In 1934 a specification was issued for a more capable light *Landwirtschaftschlepper* as a stop gap until the development of a definitive battle tank for the *Panzertruppen* could be completed. A MAN design was chosen. Variants produced up to 1940 were as follows.

Ausf a first 100 vehicles built 1935-6. These were fitted with a suspension of six small road wheels each side sprung in pairs between the sides of the tank and an outside girder. There were three sub-types with minor improvements to the transmission and 130 h.p. Maybach HL51TR petrol engine. Details were: weight 7.2 tonnes, road speed 40 k.p.h., road range 210 km, cross country range 160 km. Armour was 14.5mm all round.

Ausf b this model of which up to 100 were built in 1936-7 had the 140 h.p. Maybach HL62TR engine, revised gearbox and the nose armour thickened to 30mm. Weight was now 7.9 tonnes, road range 190 km and cross country range 125 km.

Ausf c final development model built 1937. This introduced the definitive suspension of five large elliptically sprung road wheels each side. Weight was 8.8 tonnes.

Ausf A first definitive production version was introduced in 1937 with a more easily produced squared off nose armoured to 34.5mm with extra 20mm armour on the

Left: The victor in Paris. In the shadow of the Eiffel Tower a German soldier on air sentry duty keeps watch.

driver's plate and turret front. This increased weight to 9.5 tonnes; an improved HL62TRM engine was fitted.

Ausf B introduced a turret cupola for the commander replacing the original hatches and periscope.

Ausf C as for Ausf B but with detail differences such as thicker observation glass. Production petered out in March 1940.

Ausf D and E special version developed as a *Schnelkampfwagen* (Fast Fighting Vehicle) for the tank battalions of the light divisions. The layout of the hull was altered and these tanks had a completely new suspension of four large, torsion bar suspended, road wheels each side which increased the road speed to 55 k.p.h. Road range was also up to 200 km, 130 km cross country. A new transmission was fitted and armour was 30mm maximum. About 250 of these 10 tonne tanks were built in 1938-9, the last as Ausf E with strengthened torsion bars. These were not successful vehicles having a disappointing cross country performance and do not appear to have seen much service with the Light Divisions. They were also used by 4th Panzer Brigade.

All PzKpfw II models were armed with one 20mm KwK30 and one 7.92mm MG34 machine-gun in the turret. The crew was three. Builders were MAN, Daimler, Famo, Wegmann, MIAG, Henschel and Alkett.

PzKpfw III (SdKfz 141)

Work on a larger 15 tonne tank for the 'light' companies of the Panzer battalions began in 1934 and the Daimler Benz prototype was chosen for development. By 1940 there were six models in existence of what had begun under the pseudonym *Zugführerwagen* (Platoon Commander's Vehicle).

Ausf A The first ten trial vehicles produced in 1936-7 with a distinctive suspension of five large coil sprung road wheels each side with only two return rollers. The engine was a Maybach HL108TR of 250 h.p. with only 14.5mm armour, weight was 15.4 tonnes; maximum road speed 32 k.p.h., road range 165 km and cross country range 95 km.

Ausf B This development version tried a new suspension with two large leaf springs, eight small bogie wheels and three return rollers. Weight was increased to 15.9 tonnes. Twelve were built in 1937-8. Road speed was marginally increased to 35 k.p.h.

Ausf C Slightly modified version of the above suspension with one large spring for the two centre bogie wheel pairs and a separate spring for the pairs at each end. Up to 15 of these were built concurrently with the Ausf B.

Ausf D Had a similar suspension to the C but with angled front and rear springs. They also had the armour on the front and sides of the hull and turret increased to 30mm thickness putting up the weight to 19.8 tonnes. A new turret cupola and modified transmission were fitted. Up to 30 of these tanks were built in 1938 and the older pre-production vehicles were brought up to this new standard and redesignated Ausf D, although they retained their original suspensions and cupolas.

Ausf E This model finally arrived at the definitive suspension with six road wheels each side suspended by torsion bars. A more powerful 300 h.p. HL120TR engine was adopted together with a complicated and advanced transmission. The design of the driver's plate was also revised. Forty-one appear to have been built in 1939.

Ausf F The first quantity production version, built in 1939, distinguished by new ventilation covers for the track brakes on the upper nose plate. The Ausf F was also fitted with the slightly modified HL120TRM engine.

Ausf G The main 1940 production variant. Redesigned driver's plate. Most had new improved cupola and re-shaped turret rear.

Until the beginning of the French campaign all PzKpfw IIIs were armed with one turret mounted 45 calibre 37mm KwK with two co-axial 7.92mm MG34 machine-guns. An extra MG34 was in the hull front. During the French campaign the new 42 calibre 50mm KwK appeared. Their turrets had an external mantlet with single MG34 and other small changes. Crew on all models was five. Builders of the PzKpfw III from 1936 to 1940 were Daimler Benz, Alkett, Wegmann, Henschel, MAN, FAMO and MNH.

PzKpfw IV (SdKfz 161)

Development contracts were issued in 1934 for a gun support medium tank for the proposed Panzer battalions. The *Bataillonführerwagen* (Battalion Leader's Vehicle) had already begun in 1930 and in 1935 Krupp was given the task of producing a successful tank from the various available designs. There were six versions of PzKpfw IV available by 1940.

Ausf A First limited production version which introduced the definitive suspension of eight small road wheels, leaf sprung in pairs each side with four return rollers. The engine was a Maybach HL108TR of 230 h.p. nominal rating. Armour was 14.5mm on the hull, 20mm on the turret and the tank weighed 17.3 tonnes. Maximum road speed was 30 k.p.h., road range 150 km and cross country range 100 km. Thirty-five were constructed 1937-8.

Ausf B Introduced heavier 30mm frontal hull armour, straight driver's plate and new cupola. The 300 h.p. HL120TR engine was fitted. Weight was 17.7 tonnes, road speed 40 k.p.h., road range 200 km and cross country range 130 km. Forty-two were built in 1938.

Ausf C As Ausf B but with 30 mm armour extended to the turret front. Weight was 20 tonnes. In 1938-9 140 were built and this was the major single PzKpfw IV type in service in Poland and France. Late production vehicles had the Maybach HL120TRM engine.

Ausf D Built in 1939-40 this reverted to a stepped driver's plate design with hull machine-gun. Side armour was increased to 20mm and the turret guns were mounted in an external mantlet.

All PzKpfw IV models were armed with a 24 calibre 75mm KwK and a 7.92mm MG34 machine-gun in the turret. Ausf A and D-F also had an extra MG34 in the driver's plate. Crew of all models was five and in this period PzKpfw IV were built only by Krupp.

Neubaufahrzeug

In 1933 a specification was issued to Rheinmentall Borsig to develop a multi-turreted heavy tank. Two soft steel prototypes were built the next year armed with a 23.5 calibre 75mm gun in the main turret together with a 45 calibre 37mm gun above it and an MG13 machine-gun to the side. There was a similar weapon in each of the two auxiliary turrets. The main turret design was not satisfactory and Krupp built a new design for the three armoured prototype chassis when they appeared in 1934. This turret mounted the two main guns side by side. Machine-gun armament was as before. A 280 h.p. Maybach HL108TR engine was fitted. Maximum armour thickness was 20mm and the tanks weighed 23 tonnes. Maximum road speed was 30 k.p.h. and the crew was six. Clumsier than the comparable PzKpfw IV the NbFz had no place in a *Blitzkrieg* army and further development was abandoned.

PzKpfw 35(t)

This was the Czech Army's LT-35 tank, a joint Skoda/CKDSIIa development of the Skoda SII design which had proved something of a failure on its trials due to its advanced and unreliable pneumatically assisted steering and gear change. The problems were never entirely ironed out but, when it worked, the system greatly eased the strain on the driver. The improved tank was accepted for service in the Czech Army in 1936. A good leaf sprung suspension of two sets of double bogie wheel pairs each side equalised wear and gave long track life. The engine was a 120 h.p. Skoda T-11. Maximum road speed was 40 k.p.h., road range 200 km and cross country range 115 km. Armament was one turret mounted 40 calibre 37.2mm Skoda A3 gun with a 7.92mm MG37(t) and another MG37(t) in the left hull front. The riveted armour was 28-35mm thick on the front, 16-24mm on the sides. The crew was four and the tanks were built by both Skoda and CKD (later BMM).

PzKpfw 38(t)

In the mid 1930's CKD/Praga developed a strong but simple suspension of four large elliptically sprung road wheels each side for a series of light tanks aimed at the export market. The TNH was adopted for the Czech Army as the LT-38. Production was continued by the Germans at BMM and there were various small differences between sub-types but all had 125 h.p. Praga EPA engines, 25mm frontal armour and 15-19mm protection on the sides. Armament was one turret mounted 47.8 calibre 37.2mm Skoda A7 gun with a 7.92mm MG37(t) machine-gun alongside and a similar weapon in the hull front. The crew was four and performance figures were road speed 42 k.p.h., road range 200 km, cross country range 140 km.

Panzerbefehlswagen

In order to provide maximum mobility for Panzer command echelons 'leading from the front' at all levels from battalion to brigade a number of specialised command tanks were built of two basic types.

Kleiner Panzerbefehlswagen (SdKfz 265) Up to 200 of these were built on the PzKpfw I chassis, a few earlier vehicles on the Ausf A but most utilising the Ausf B. The latter had a high eight sided superstructure for three-man crew, map tables and Fu6 and Fu2 radios which allowed short range communication at all divisional levels. A single MG34 was carried in the superstructure front.

Grosser Panzerbefehlswagen Built on pre-production PzKpfw III chassis, first Ausf D (PzBefWg III Ausf A) and then Ausf E (PzBefWg III Ausf B) completed in 1940 the latter had many features similar to the Ausf G combat tank. There were three versions of each type: SdKfz 266 with the same radios as the Kleiner PzBefWg; SkDfz 267 for higher echelons carrying the Fu6 and Fu8 for longer range up to 40 km communication with divisional H.Q.; SdKfz 268 with the Fu6 and Fu7 allowing contact with aircraft up to 50 km for co-ordinating close air support. The turrets of these vehicles were fixed and had a dummy gun fitted to allow extra space for map tables, radios and the five man crew. A single MG34 was carried. About 15 Ausf A had appeared by the outbreak of war with about 30 more Ausf A and B becoming available by May 1940.